Eyewitness
CAR

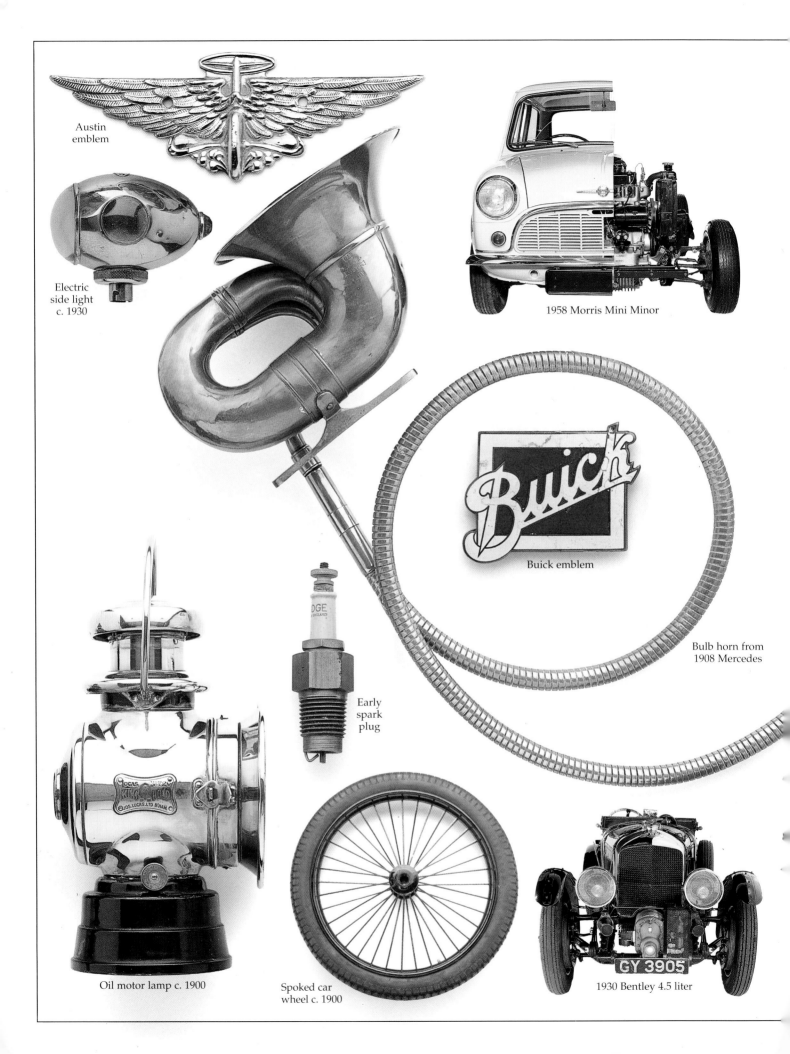

Austin emblem

Electric side light c. 1930

1958 Morris Mini Minor

Buick emblem

Bulb horn from 1908 Mercedes

Early spark plug

Oil motor lamp c. 1900

Spoked car wheel c. 1900

1930 Bentley 4.5 liter

Headlight bulbs c. 1900

Ferrari emblem

Eyewitness
CAR

Written by
RICHARD SUTTON

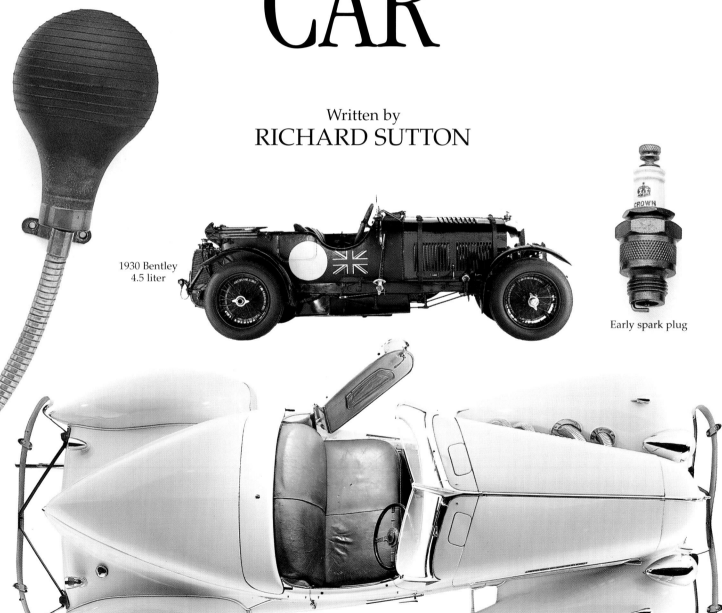

1930 Bentley
4.5 liter

Early spark plug

1935 Auburn 951 Speedster

DK Publishing, Inc.

Fuel injector

Steering rack

DK

**LONDON, NEW YORK, MUNICH,
MELBOURNE, and DELHI**

Project editor John Farndon
Design Mathewson Bull
Managing editor Sophie Mitchell
Senior art editor Julie Harris
Editorial director Sue Unstead
Art director Anne-Marie Bulat

REVISED EDITION
Editors Barbara Berger, Laura Buller
Editorial assistant John Searcy
Publishing director Beth Sutinis
Senior designer Tai Blanche
Designers Jessica Lasher, Diana Catherines
Photo research Chrissy McIntyre
Art director Dirk Kaufman
DTP designer Milos Orlovic
Production Ivor Parker

This Eyewitness ® Guide has been conceived by
Dorling Kindersley Limited and Editions Gallimard

This edition published in the United States in 2005
by DK Publishing, Inc.
375 Hudson Street, New York, NY 10014

05 06 07 08 09 10 9 8 7 6 5 4 3 2 1

A catalog record for this book is
available from the Library of Congress.

ISBN 0-7566-1384-1 (Hardcover) 0-7566-1393-0 (Library Binding)

Color reproduction by Colourscan, Singapore
Printed in China by Toppan Printing Co.,
(Shenzhen) Ltd.

Discover more at
www.dk.com

Telescopic
shock absorber
and coil spring

Early spark plugs

Contents

Early spark plugs

Horseless power

ONE AFTERNOON in the summer of 1862, a Frenchman named Étienne Lenoir gingerly started the engine he had built and mounted between the wheels of an old horse cart. Minutes later, the little cart was trundling through the Vincennes forest near Paris, moved only by the slowly thumping engine. It was a historic moment, for Lenoir's self-propelled cart was launched into a world of horsedrawn carriages and stagecoaches, cart tracks and dust roads – a world that would soon vanish forever. Lenoir was not the first to build a "horseless carriage"; carriages powered by cumbersome steam engines had already been made for almost a century. His breakthrough was the invention of the compact "internal combustion" engine (pp. 42-45), which worked by burning gas inside a cylinder. A few years later, these engines were made to run on gasoline and soon the first experimental motor cars were being built. In 1885, the first car to be sold to the public rolled out of the workshops of Karl Benz in Mannheim in Germany. The age of the automobile had begun.

THE FIRST CAR SOLD
Dating from 1888, this is an ad for the first car ever sold, Karl Benz's three-wheeler "Patent-Motorwagen."

MAKING A DASH FOR IT
The front panel of many early cars was reminiscent of the "dashboard" of the horse carriage – so-called because it saved the coachman from being "dashed" by flying stones thrown up by the horses. Even today, a car's instrument panel is still referred to as the dash.

COACH SPRING
Early cars had curved iron springs to smooth the ride – just like those used on horse coaches throughout the 19th century.

Coach spring

Engine

COACHWORK
The first motor cars owed a great deal to the horse carriage. Indeed, many pioneering cars were simply horse carts with an engine – which is one reason they were known as horseless carriages. Even purpose-built cars were usually made by a traditional coachbuilder, using centuries-old skills and techniques.

TAKE AWAY THE HORSE . . .
The similarities between horse carriages and the first cars are obvious. Note the large wheels, boat-shaped body, high driver's seat, and dashboard.

HILL-CLIMBING
Many early cars could not climb hills because they had no gears; they simply came to a standstill and then rolled backward. But on the Benz Victoria of 1890, the driver was given a lever to slip the leather drive belt onto a small pulley. This meant the wheels turned more slowly, but the extra leverage enabled the car to climb uphill. The chain-driven Velo had three of these forward-gear pulleys and one reverse.

HORSE SENSE
The first cars were notoriously unreliable. This cartoon suggested it might be just as well to take a couple of horses along in case of a breakdown.

Massive flywheel to keep the engine running smoothly

Rear wheels driven by chains looped arwound big cogs on either wheel

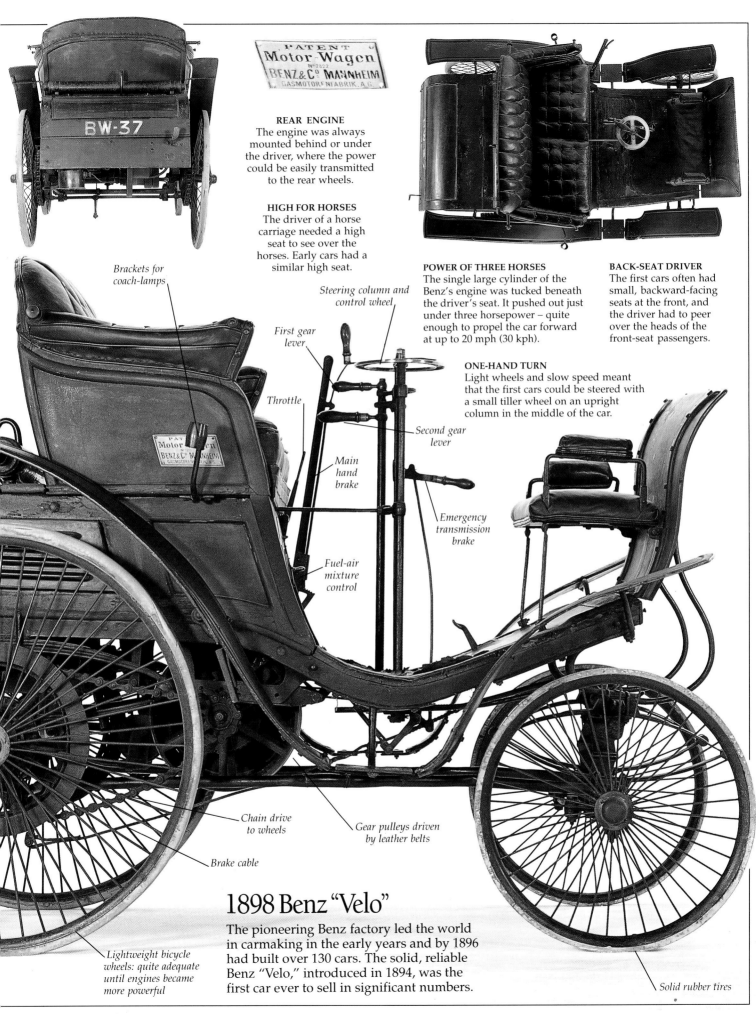

PATENT Motor-Wagen BENZ & Cº MANNHEIM GASMOTORENFABRIK. A.G.

BW-37

REAR ENGINE
The engine was always mounted behind or under the driver, where the power could be easily transmitted to the rear wheels.

HIGH FOR HORSES
The driver of a horse carriage needed a high seat to see over the horses. Early cars had a similar high seat.

POWER OF THREE HORSES
The single large cylinder of the Benz's engine was tucked beneath the driver's seat. It pushed out just under three horsepower – quite enough to propel the car forward at up to 20 mph (30 kph).

BACK-SEAT DRIVER
The first cars often had small, backward-facing seats at the front, and the driver had to peer over the heads of the front-seat passengers.

ONE-HAND TURN
Light wheels and slow speed meant that the first cars could be steered with a small tiller wheel on an upright column in the middle of the car.

Brackets for coach-lamps

Steering column and control wheel

First gear lever

Throttle

Second gear lever

Main hand brake

Emergency transmission brake

Fuel-air mixture control

Chain drive to wheels

Gear pulleys driven by leather belts

Brake cable

Lightweight bicycle wheels: quite adequate until engines became more powerful

Solid rubber tires

1898 Benz "Velo"

The pioneering Benz factory led the world in carmaking in the early years and by 1896 had built over 130 cars. The solid, reliable Benz "Velo," introduced in 1894, was the first car ever to sell in significant numbers.

The pioneers

By 1900, CARS WERE LOOKING MORE LIKE CARS and less like horse carriages. The pioneering cars were difficult to start, and even more difficult to drive. But each year new ideas made the car a more practical and useful machine. In France, carmakers such as Panhard Levassor, De Dion Bouton, and Renault were especially inventive. It was Panhard who thought of putting the engine at the front and who, in 1895, built the first sedan. Renault championed the idea of a shaft, rather than a chain, to drive the rear wheels. In the early 1900s, the French roadsters were by far the most popular cars in Europe. Everywhere, though, the car was making progress. In the United States, where the Duryea brothers had made the first successful American car in 1893, cars such as the famous Oldsmobile Curved Dash were selling by the thousand. In Britain in 1900, 23 cars completed a 1,000-mile (1,600-km) run from London to Scotland and back.

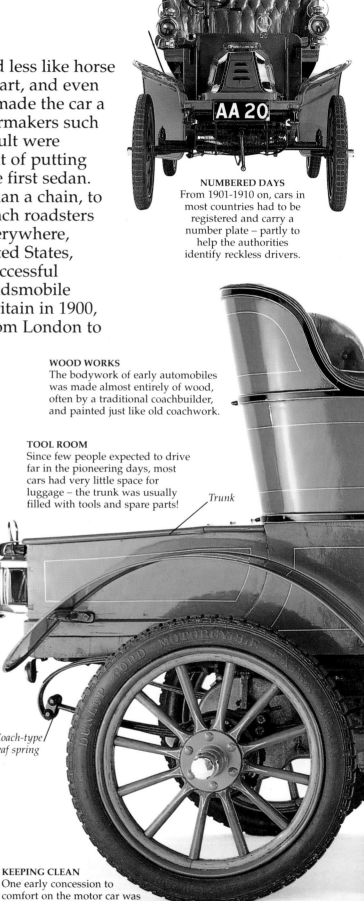

NUMBERED DAYS
From 1901-1910 on, cars in most countries had to be registered and carry a number plate – partly to help the authorities identify reckless drivers.

WOOD WORKS
The bodywork of early automobiles was made almost entirely of wood, often by a traditional coachbuilder, and painted just like old coachwork.

TOOL ROOM
Since few people expected to drive far in the pioneering days, most cars had very little space for luggage – the trunk was usually filled with tools and spare parts!

Trunk

INFERNAL MACHINES
The arrival of the first cars in country towns and villages created quite a stir. But they were not always welcome, for they scared horses and threw up thick clouds of dust.

"GET OUT AND GET UNDER!"
Breakdowns marred many a day out in the early years – and even inspired a famous music hall song. Here the mechanic has removed the front seat – probably to get at the troublesome transmission. But such mishaps were already less common in 1903 than they had been five years earlier.

Coach-type leaf spring

KEEPING CLEAN
One early concession to comfort on the motor car was the addition of mudguards around the wheels to protect passengers from dirt thrown up off the roads.

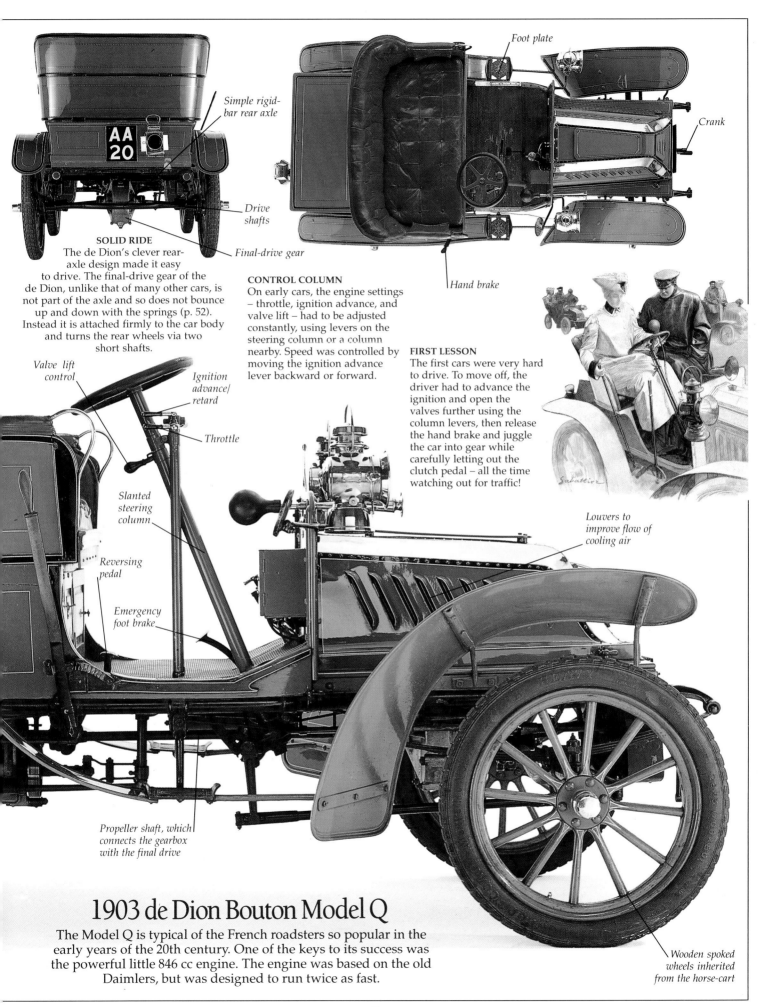

Simple rigid-bar rear axle

AA 20

Drive shafts

Final-drive gear

Foot plate

Crank

Hand brake

SOLID RIDE
The de Dion's clever rear-axle design made it easy to drive. The final-drive gear of the de Dion, unlike that of many other cars, is not part of the axle and so does not bounce up and down with the springs (p. 52). Instead it is attached firmly to the car body and turns the rear wheels via two short shafts.

CONTROL COLUMN
On early cars, the engine settings – throttle, ignition advance, and valve lift – had to be adjusted constantly, using levers on the steering column or a column nearby. Speed was controlled by moving the ignition advance lever backward or forward.

FIRST LESSON
The first cars were very hard to drive. To move off, the driver had to advance the ignition and open the valves further using the column levers, then release the hand brake and juggle the car into gear while carefully letting out the clutch pedal – all the time watching out for traffic!

Valve lift control

Ignition advance/ retard

Throttle

Slanted steering column

Reversing pedal

Emergency foot brake

Louvers to improve flow of cooling air

Propeller shaft, which connects the gearbox with the final drive

Wooden spoked wheels inherited from the horse-cart

1903 de Dion Bouton Model Q

The Model Q is typical of the French roadsters so popular in the early years of the 20th century. One of the keys to its success was the powerful little 846 cc engine. The engine was based on the old Daimlers, but was designed to run twice as fast.

Warning signals

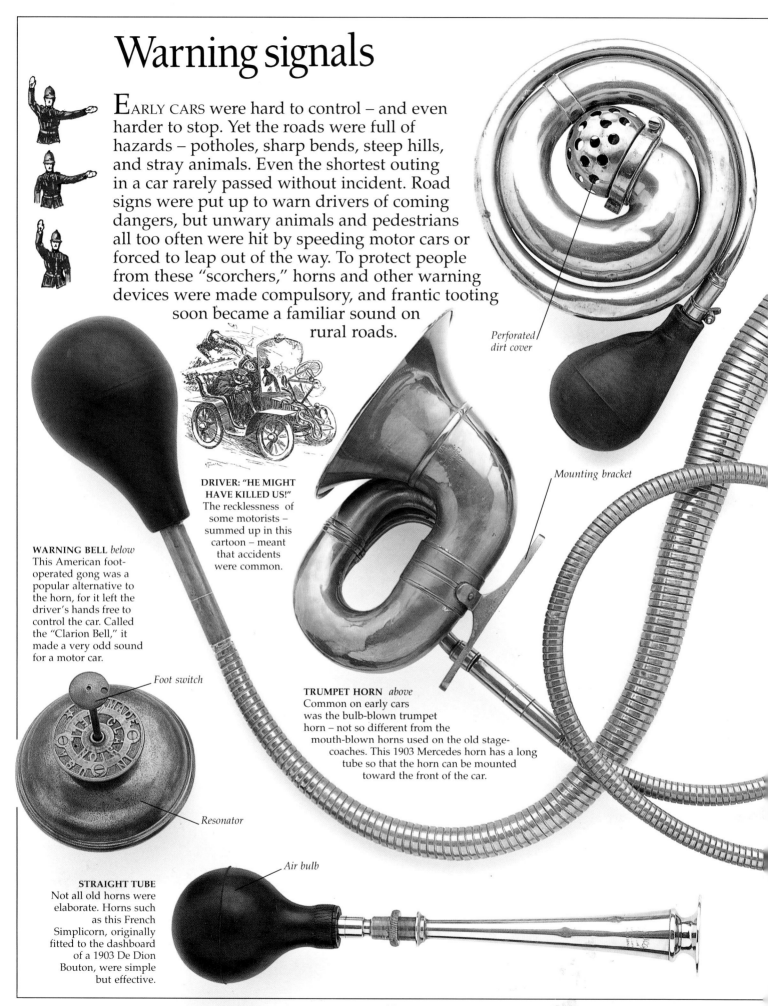

EARLY CARS were hard to control – and even harder to stop. Yet the roads were full of hazards – potholes, sharp bends, steep hills, and stray animals. Even the shortest outing in a car rarely passed without incident. Road signs were put up to warn drivers of coming dangers, but unwary animals and pedestrians all too often were hit by speeding motor cars or forced to leap out of the way. To protect people from these "scorchers," horns and other warning devices were made compulsory, and frantic tooting soon became a familiar sound on rural roads.

Perforated dirt cover

DRIVER: "HE MIGHT HAVE KILLED US!"
The recklessness of some motorists – summed up in this cartoon – meant that accidents were common.

WARNING BELL *below*
This American foot-operated gong was a popular alternative to the horn, for it left the driver's hands free to control the car. Called the "Clarion Bell," it made a very odd sound for a motor car.

Mounting bracket

Foot switch

Resonator

TRUMPET HORN *above*
Common on early cars was the bulb-blown trumpet horn – not so different from the mouth-blown horns used on the old stage-coaches. This 1903 Mercedes horn has a long tube so that the horn can be mounted toward the front of the car.

Air bulb

STRAIGHT TUBE
Not all old horns were elaborate. Horns such as this French Simplicorn, originally fitted to the dashboard of a 1903 De Dion Bouton, were simple but effective.

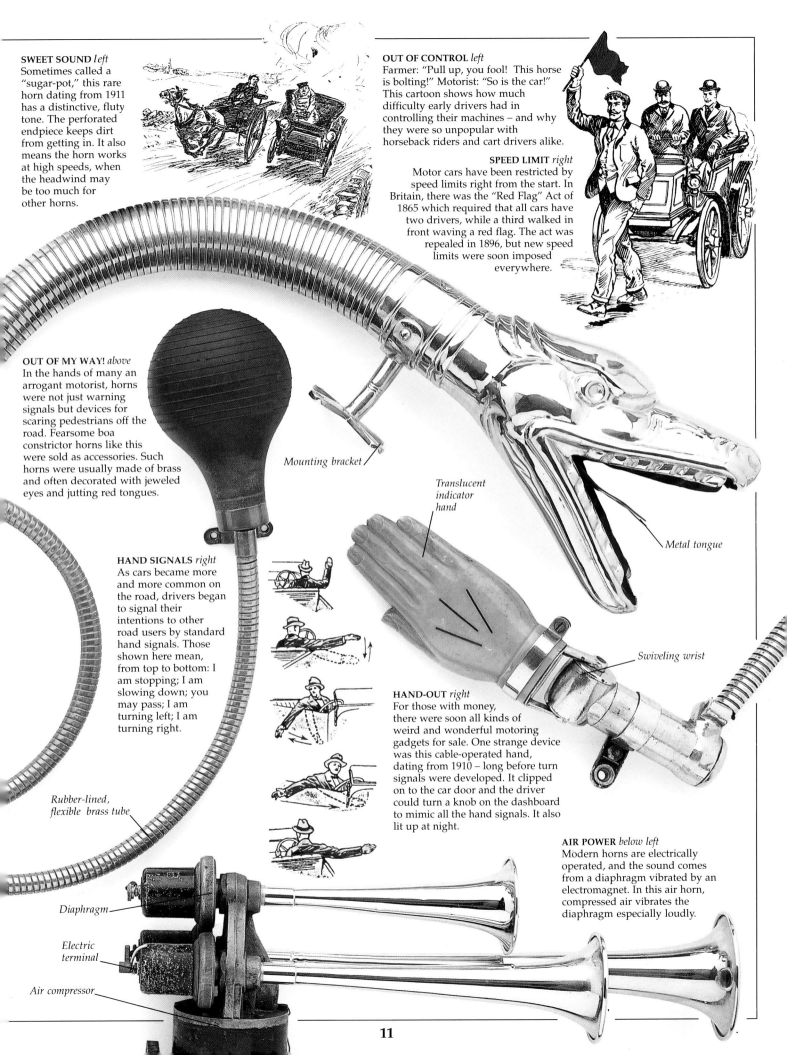

SWEET SOUND *left*
Sometimes called a "sugar-pot," this rare horn dating from 1911 has a distinctive, fluty tone. The perforated endpiece keeps dirt from getting in. It also means the horn works at high speeds, when the headwind may be too much for other horns.

OUT OF CONTROL *left*
Farmer: "Pull up, you fool! This horse is bolting!" Motorist: "So is the car!" This cartoon shows how much difficulty early drivers had in controlling their machines – and why they were so unpopular with horseback riders and cart drivers alike.

SPEED LIMIT *right*
Motor cars have been restricted by speed limits right from the start. In Britain, there was the "Red Flag" Act of 1865 which required that all cars have two drivers, while a third walked in front waving a red flag. The act was repealed in 1896, but new speed limits were soon imposed everywhere.

OUT OF MY WAY! *above*
In the hands of many an arrogant motorist, horns were not just warning signals but devices for scaring pedestrians off the road. Fearsome boa constrictor horns like this were sold as accessories. Such horns were usually made of brass and often decorated with jeweled eyes and jutting red tongues.

Mounting bracket

Translucent indicator hand

Metal tongue

HAND SIGNALS *right*
As cars became more and more common on the road, drivers began to signal their intentions to other road users by standard hand signals. Those shown here mean, from top to bottom: I am stopping; I am slowing down; you may pass; I am turning left; I am turning right.

Swiveling wrist

HAND-OUT *right*
For those with money, there were soon all kinds of weird and wonderful motoring gadgets for sale. One strange device was this cable-operated hand, dating from 1910 – long before turn signals were developed. It clipped on to the car door and the driver could turn a knob on the dashboard to mimic all the hand signals. It also lit up at night.

Rubber-lined, flexible brass tube

AIR POWER *below left*
Modern horns are electrically operated, and the sound comes from a diaphragm vibrated by an electromagnet. In this air horn, compressed air vibrates the diaphragm especially loudly.

Diaphragm

Electric terminal

Air compressor

Coachbuilt splendor

Elegant women and their uniformed chauffeurs became the subject of many a romantic story

As CARS BECAME CHEAPER and more popular, so the rich wanted more and more exclusive automobiles. The luxury cars of the pre-World War I years were made with the best technology and the best craftsmanship. No expense was spared, and these luxury autos – Hispano-Suizas, Benzes, Delauney-Belvilles, and Rolls-Royces – were built to standards rarely seen again in carmaking. Interiors were furnished with velvet and brocade, fine leather and thick pile carpets. Bodies were made precisely to the customers' requirements by the finest coachbuilders. The engines were large, powerful, and smooth-running. But they were cars not for the rich to drive, but to be driven in, by professional chauffeurs or drivers.

FASHIONABLE MOTORING
Rich women did not expect to drive; they simply wanted to be driven in style. One said, "I am not concerned in the least with the motor. I leave [that] to Monsieur Chauffeur. My only interest is in the interior."

OPEN CHOICE
Open tourers were often preferred to tall, closed limousines, which swayed alarmingly on corners. This one is in the style known as "Roi des Belges", after the body made for the king of Belgium's 1901 Panhard.

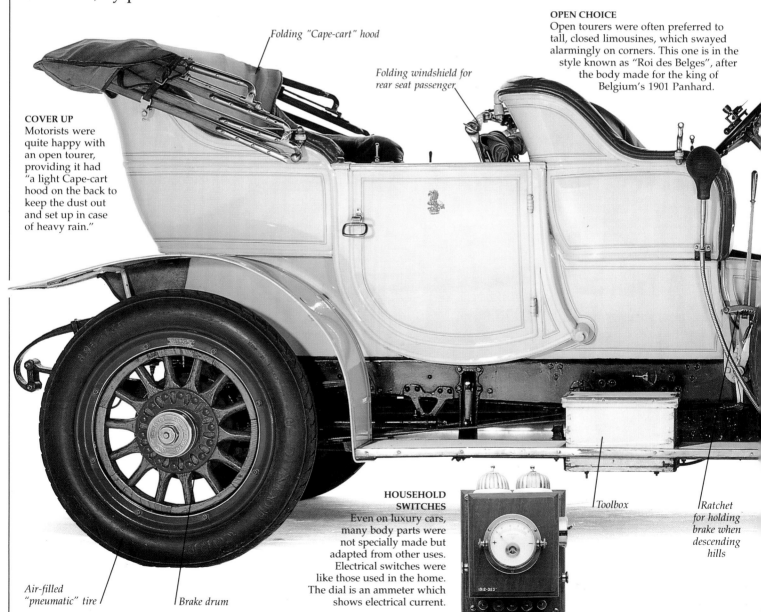

Folding "Cape-cart" hood

Folding windshield for rear seat passenger

COVER UP
Motorists were quite happy with an open tourer, providing it had "a light Cape-cart hood on the back to keep the dust out and set up in case of heavy rain."

HOUSEHOLD SWITCHES
Even on luxury cars, many body parts were not specially made but adapted from other uses. Electrical switches were like those used in the home. The dial is an ammeter which shows electrical current.

Toolbox

Ratchet for holding brake when descending hills

Air-filled "pneumatic" tire

Brake drum

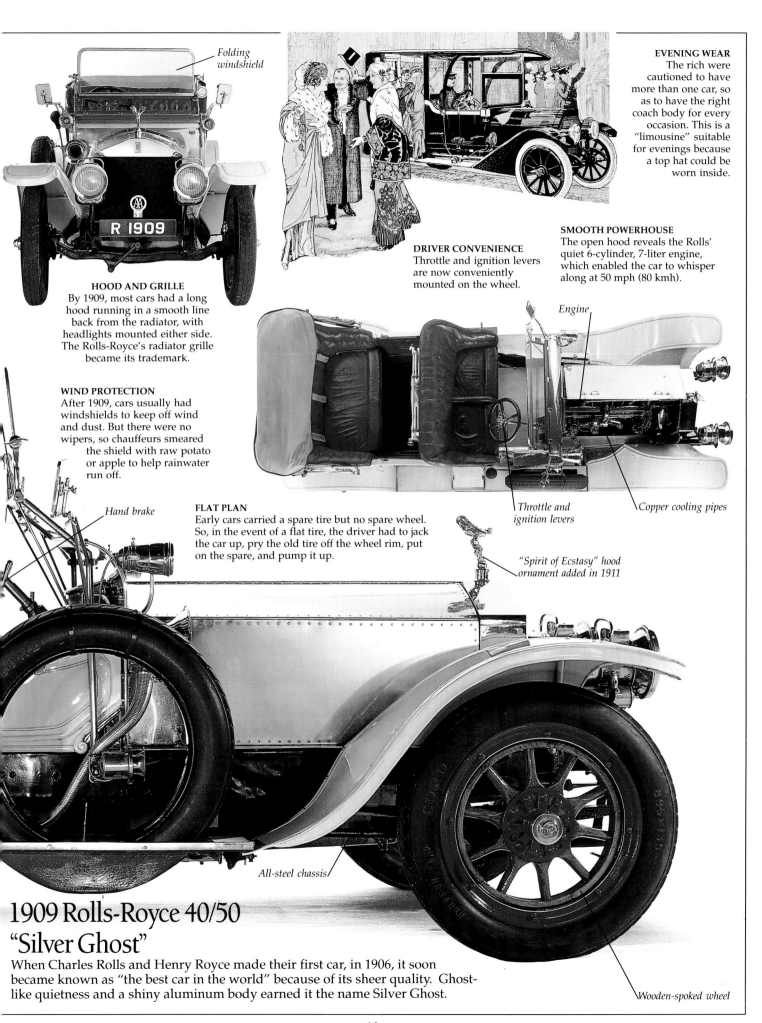

Folding windshield

EVENING WEAR
The rich were cautioned to have more than one car, so as to have the right coach body for every occasion. This is a "limousine" suitable for evenings because a top hat could be worn inside.

HOOD AND GRILLE
By 1909, most cars had a long hood running in a smooth line back from the radiator, with headlights mounted either side. The Rolls-Royce's radiator grille became its trademark.

DRIVER CONVENIENCE
Throttle and ignition levers are now conveniently mounted on the wheel.

SMOOTH POWERHOUSE
The open hood reveals the Rolls' quiet 6-cylinder, 7-liter engine, which enabled the car to whisper along at 50 mph (80 kmh).

WIND PROTECTION
After 1909, cars usually had windshields to keep off wind and dust. But there were no wipers, so chauffeurs smeared the shield with raw potato or apple to help rainwater run off.

Engine

Hand brake

FLAT PLAN
Early cars carried a spare tire but no spare wheel. So, in the event of a flat tire, the driver had to jack the car up, pry the old tire off the wheel rim, put on the spare, and pump it up.

Throttle and ignition levers

Copper cooling pipes

"Spirit of Ecstasy" hood ornament added in 1911

All-steel chassis

1909 Rolls-Royce 40/50 "Silver Ghost"

When Charles Rolls and Henry Royce made their first car, in 1906, it soon became known as "the best car in the world" because of its sheer quality. Ghost-like quietness and a shiny aluminum body earned it the name Silver Ghost.

Wooden-spoked wheel

The open road

Owning a car provided every reason for dressing up and getting equipped for touring. Indeed, protective clothing was vital in the open cars of the pioneer era. Not only was there rain and cold to contend with but, worst of all, the dreadful dust thrown up by dry dirt roads. Motorists would often come home covered from head to foot in a thick layer of muck. At first, clothes were adapted from riding and yachting and other outdoor pursuits. But before long a huge variety of special motoring clothes was on sale. Some were practical and sensible; others clearly for show. A motorist could easily spend as much on a motoring wardrobe as on a new car. Yet the pleasures of the open road made all the little hardships and the expense worthwhile, and touring became highly fashionable.

Nose-swivel to insure good fit

Orange tint to reduce road glare

Dust flap for ears

THE RIGHT GEAR
Goggles and headgear were vital in an open car with no windshield. At first, peaked caps (right) were popular with the fashion-conscious; serious drivers preferred helmet and goggles (left and above). But soon most drivers were wearing helmets – with built-in visors, earmuffs, and even "anti-collision protectors."

DRESSED TO DRIVE *above*
Here are just some of the many styles of early motoring wear. The woman's "beekeeper" bonnet was very popular with fashionable women for keeping dust off the face and hair. Thick fur coats were usually made at huge expense from Russian sable, ocelot, and beaver.

Copper body to conduct heat

HANDY WEAR
The driver's hands would soon get cold and dirty on the controls. So a good pair of gloves – preferably gauntlets – was essential. Gauntlets were usually fur-lined leather, like many modern motorcycle gloves.

HOT FOOT
Sitting in an open car on a winter's day could make one bitterly cold. Many a passenger must have been grateful for a foot-warmer like this, which could be filled with hot water before setting out. Foot muffs and "puttees" (leggings) also helped keep out the cold.

Heatproof felt

TEA BAG *left*
With few roadside cafés, British motorists found taking their own tea with them was a necessity – and all part of the great adventure of motoring. Since the journey could take hours, and you could be stranded anywhere, it was worth doing properly. So motorists paid for beautiful tea baskets like this one in leather and silver. They often came with a matching lunch basket.

Tea box

Combined kettle and teapot

PICNIC BY THE SEA
Only the rich could afford a car in the early days, so motoring picnics tended to be lavish. The luxury shops could provide fine cutlery and glass, as well as hampers of champagne, roast chicken, and other expensive food.

Paraffin stove to heat water   Matchbox

THE JOYS OF MOTORING *left*
Car advertisements made the most of the pleasures of fast motoring through lovely countryside. This is a picture of a 6-cylinder Essex, a typical 1920s American sedan.

WHERE NEXT? *right*
Getting lost became a regular hazard for pioneer motorists on tour. Signposts were then few and far between. One dirt road looked much like another. And there was no coachman on hand to guide the motorist safely home. Sets of the new, detailed road maps that quickly appeared in stores became as vital to the motorist as a set of tools.

Complete set of road maps in leather index case, from the 1920s

Mass-production

Cars were the toys of the rich in the early days. But it was Detroit farmboy Henry Ford's dream to build "a motor car for the great multitude – a car so low in price that no man making a good salary will be unable to own one." When he finally realized his dream, with the launch of the Model T Ford in 1908, the effect was revolutionary. The T meant people barely able to afford a horse and buggy could buy a car. In 1908, fewer than 200,000 people in the U.S. owned cars; five years later 250,000 owned Model Ts alone. By 1930, over 15 million Ts had been sold. The key to Ford's success was mass production. By using huge teams of men working systematically to build huge numbers of cars, he could sell them all very cheaply. Indeed, the more he sold, the cheaper they became.

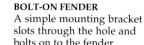

BOLT-ON FENDER
A simple mounting bracket slots through the hole and bolts on to the fender.

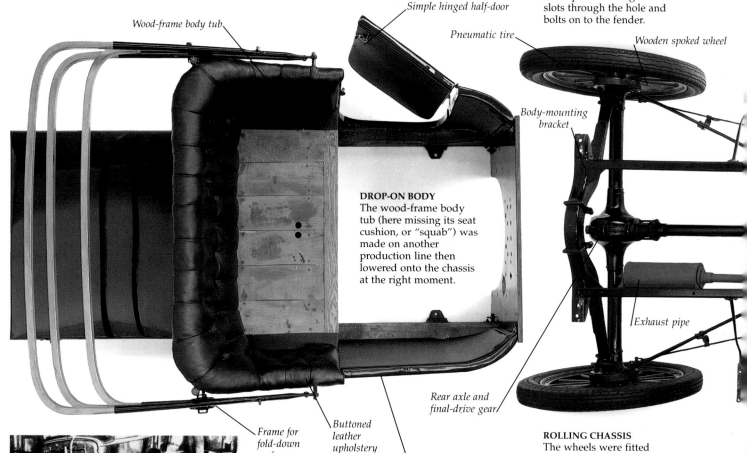

Wood-frame body tub

Simple hinged half-door

Pneumatic tire

Wooden spoked wheel

Body-mounting bracket

DROP-ON BODY
The wood-frame body tub (here missing its seat cushion, or "squab") was made on another production line then lowered onto the chassis at the right moment.

Exhaust pipe

Frame for fold-down roof

Buttoned leather upholstery

Rear axle and final-drive gear

Pressed steel body panel

ROLLING CHASSIS
The wheels were fitted early in production so that the chassis could be easily moved.

The production line

Before Ford, complete cars were built by small teams of men. In the Ford factory, each worker added just one small component, as partly assembled cars were pulled rapidly past on the production line.

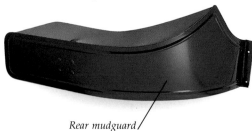

Rear mudguard

HENRY FORD AND SON
The principles Ford used to make the Model T are used in car manufacturing to this day. Modern assembly lines use robots to build cars more quickly, cheaply, and accurately. But the idea of assembling components on a moving production line remains.

BIT BY BIT
It is easy to see how the Model T took shape from its individual components. Fenders, running board, and sill all bolt together to form one side of the car, and are mounted directly on to the chassis.

STANDARD VARIATIONS
One of the things that made the Model T so cheap was its standardized body. At the time, most car bodies were built separately by specialist coachbuilders; the Model T's was made right on the Ford production line. So Ts could not be tailor-made to suit individual customers' requirements. Instead, Ford offered a limited variety of alternative body styles.

1909 Phaeton

1911 Roadster

1916 Doctor's coupe

1927 Tourer

STAMP COLLECTION
Before mass production, this panel would have been handmade. Ford used machines to stamp it out in a fraction of the time.

Outrigger to support bodywork

Fuel tank

Gearbox

2,898 cc engine giving top speed of 40 mph (65 kmh)

Hood

Radiator frame to support hood

Hand brake

Radiator

Right-hand-drive steering wheel

TOUGH TIN
The T's chassis appeared fragile, earning it the nickname Tin Lizzie. But it was made from vanadium steel, which proved very strong.

RUNNING REPAIRS
Simplicity and practicality were the keynotes in the T; its hood folded back or lifted right off for easy access to the engine.

Ford Model T c1912
The cheap, tough, and thoroughly reliable Model T put America, and much of the world, on the roads for the first time – and earned the affection of two whole generations of American families.

Sill

Running board

Front fender

ONLY ONE COLOR
Ford claimed that his car was available in "any color you like, so long as it's black." This meant painting was cheap and simple. Later models came in other colors.

Supercharged power

IN THE 1920s, many motorists owned powerful new "sports" cars – cars made purely for the pleasure of driving fast. The sports cars of the 1920s had huge engines and devices such as superchargers to give them an extra turn of speed. A few cars, including the Duesenberg J and the Bentley, could top 100 mph (160 kmh). Sports cars like these often had an impressive racing pedigree, for manufacturers were aware of the publicity to be won from success in auto racing. Alfa Romeo, Bugatti, Bentley, Chevrolet, and Duesenberg all earned their reputations on the racetrack. And technical innovations made to win races were quickly put into cars for the ordinary motorist; the Bentley sold to the public was little different from its racing counterpart.

ONLY THE BRAVEST
A Delage speeds above the famous red line at Montlhery near Paris. To run so high on the banked track, cars had to go over 90 mph (150 kmh).

BACK-SEAT RACERS
To bridge the gap between road cars and racing cars, some races in the 1920s were closed to all but four-seater tourers. The famous 24-hour event at Le Mans in France was such a race – which is why this Bentley had a back seat.

SINGLE EXIT
The Bentley has only one front door, for the benefit of the co-driver. On the driver's side, there is simply a dip in the bodywork to make the outside hand brake easy to reach.

1930 Bentley 4.5 liter supercharged

A series of sensational victories in the Le Mans 24-hour races in 1924, 1927, 1928, 1929, and 1930 made the big Bentleys legendary.

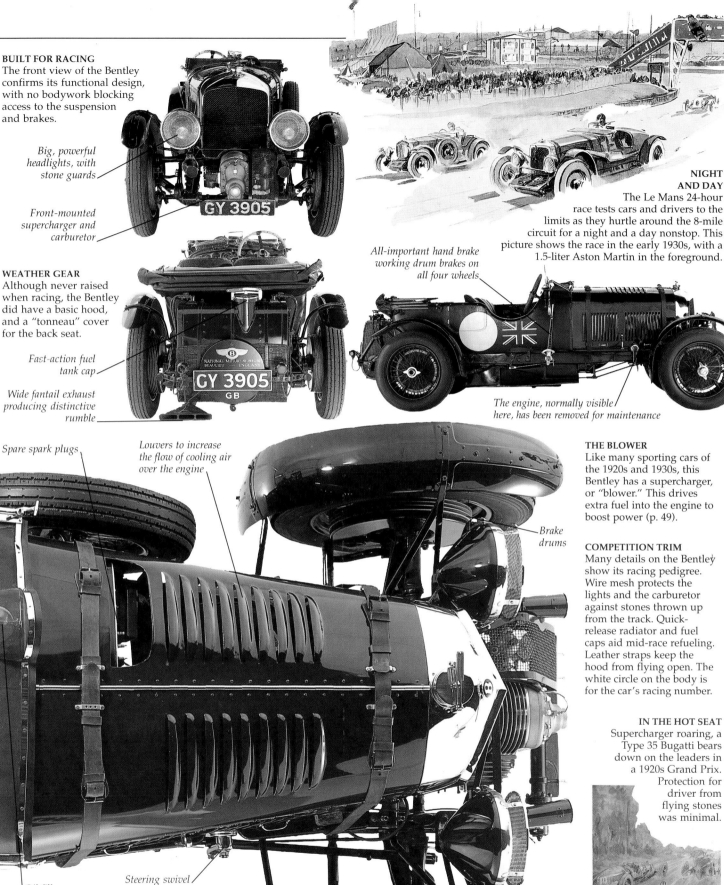

BUILT FOR RACING
The front view of the Bentley confirms its functional design, with no bodywork blocking access to the suspension and brakes.

Big, powerful headlights, with stone guards

Front-mounted supercharger and carburetor

GY 3905

WEATHER GEAR
Although never raised when racing, the Bentley did have a basic hood, and a "tonneau" cover for the back seat.

Fast-action fuel tank cap

Wide fantail exhaust producing distinctive rumble

NATIONAL MOTOR MUSEUM
BEAULIEU   ENGLAND
GY 3905
GB

All-important hand brake working drum brakes on all four wheels

NIGHT AND DAY
The Le Mans 24-hour race tests cars and drivers to the limits as they hurtle around the 8-mile circuit for a night and a day nonstop. This picture shows the race in the early 1930s, with a 1.5-liter Aston Martin in the foreground.

The engine, normally visible here, has been removed for maintenance

Spare spark plugs

Louvers to increase the flow of cooling air over the engine

Brake drums

THE BLOWER
Like many sporting cars of the 1920s and 1930s, this Bentley has a supercharger, or "blower." This drives extra fuel into the engine to boost power (p. 49).

COMPETITION TRIM
Many details on the Bentley show its racing pedigree. Wire mesh protects the lights and the carburetor against stones thrown up from the track. Quick-release radiator and fuel caps aid mid-race refueling. Leather straps keep the hood from flying open. The white circle on the body is for the car's racing number.

IN THE HOT SEAT
Supercharger roaring, a Type 35 Bugatti bears down on the leaders in a 1920s Grand Prix. Protection for driver from flying stones was minimal.

Oil filler cap

Steering swivel

POWER HOUSE
Superb engines, built in 3-, 4-, 4.5-, 6.5-, and 8-liter versions, made the Bentleys very quick. The supercharged 4.5-liter models could top 125 mph (200 kmh).

SUPER TRUCKS
The speed, size, and rugged, no-nonsense looks of the Bentleys provoked Italian car designer Ettore Bugatti to describe them as "the world's fastest trucks."

Lighting the way

NIGHT DRIVING today is relatively safe and easy, thanks to the power and efficiency of modern car lighting. But in the early days, lighting was so poor that few motorists ventured out on the road after dark. The lights on the first cars were candle lamps inherited from horse-drawn carriages. They were so dim that they did little more than warn other road users of the car's presence. Special car lights were soon developed, running first on oil or acetylene gas then electricity. Yet for many years lights were considered to be luxury accessories. It was not until the 1930s that bright electric lights were fitted as standard on most cars.

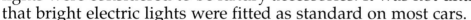

"Pie-crust" chimney top

MIDNIGHT OIL
Purpose-built lamps which burned oil or gasoline were in widespread use by 1899. The popular Lucas King of the Road "motor carriage lamp" (right) had a small red lens in the rear; separate taillights like the Miller (below) were not made compulsory until much later.

Chimney

Front lens catch to allow access for lighting the wick

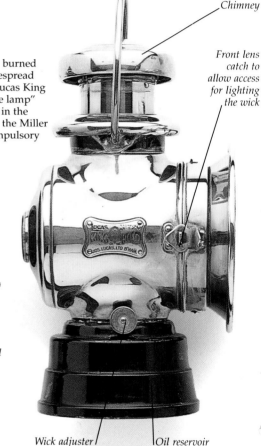

Candle wick holder

Oil reservoir

Red-stained glass lens

WAX WORKS *left*
The pioneers' cars had brackets for candle carriage lamps. Carriage lamps were beautifully made, and a spring pushed the candle up as it burned down. But dim candles were no good at all for driving. Even a slight breeze blew out the flame, while the jolting of the car shook the lamps to pieces. Candle lamps did serve a purpose, however. If the car was stranded by a breakdown at night, the lamps illuminated the immobile vehicle.

Wick adjuster

Oil reservoir

Spring-loaded candle holder

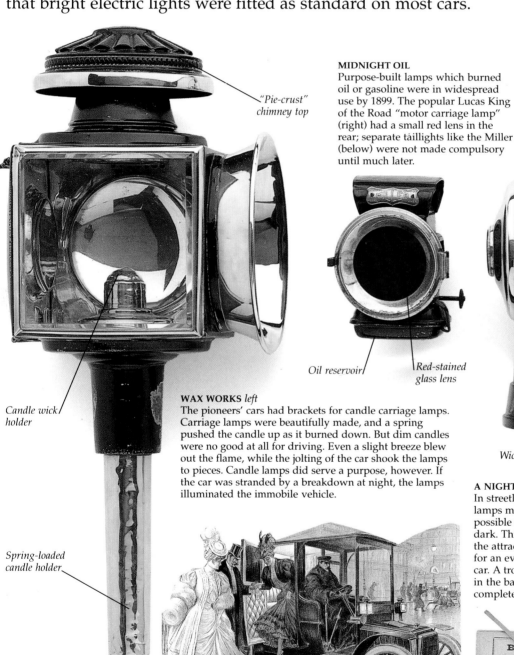

A NIGHT OUT *left*
In streetlit cities, candle lamps made it just possible to drive after dark. This ad promotes the attractions of arriving for an evening gala by car. A troublesome horse in the background completes the illusion.

BIG MATCH
Lighting a candle lamp or even an oil lamp on a windy night was a tricky business. Special strongly flaring "motor matches," made "for use on motor cars and launches," made life for the motorist a little less difficult.

ELECTRIC DREAMS
By the 1930s, electric lights were fitted as standard on most cars, and headlights – up to 13 in (33 cm) across – were included in the car's overall styling.

LIGHT RELIEF
While road surfaces were poor and bulbs still large and fragile, bulb breakage was frequent. The wise motorist always carried a full set of spares.

Early double-element "dipping" headlight bulb

OLD FLAME
The first acetylene car lamps appeared around 1898. They needed constant maintenance and occasionally exploded. But, for those who could afford them, they were much better than candles or oil, giving a steady white light, bright enough for slow driving. They remained in use until 1939.

WIRED FOR THE NIGHT
Electric car lights were first made as early as 1901. However, only in the 1920s, once cars had powerful generators, did electricity begin to take over from acetylene and night driving become practical for the first time. Electric lights have improved a lot in power and reliability since then, but few modern units match the elegant simplicity of those made by Stephen Grebel in the 1920s (below).

Acetylene supply canister

Bulb-holder supports

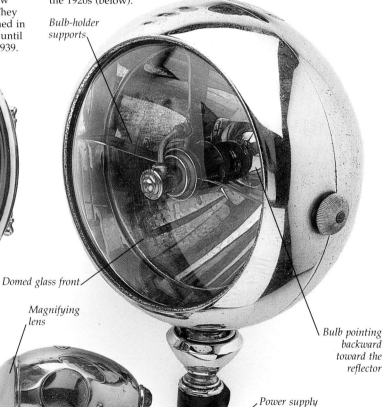

Chimney

Domed glass front

Magnifying lens

Bulb pointing backward toward the reflector

Acetylene gas burner

Glass "Mangin" mirror, curved to reflect parallel beam

Power supply

GAS SUPPLY
A familiar feature of acetylene lamps was the constant hissing of the gas generator as water dripped steadily onto solid carbide. The carbide fizzed as the water made contact, giving off a stream of acetylene gas. Sometimes the gas was made in the lamp itself; more often it was piped from a separate canister (below). New carbide had to be added every four hours or so.

Window to show light to the side

Swiveling headlights

Lucas acetylene rear lamp

LIGHT ALL AROUND
The forerunners of modern parking lights, electric lights like this were often mounted on the side of cars in the 1920s. Front, rear, and side lenses gave all-around visibility.

Headlight "dipping" lever

A QUICK DIP
Once headlights became bright enough to dazzle oncoming drivers, various ideas for interrupting the beam were tried. This one involved swiveling down ("dipping") the entire light.

Traveling in style

IF CRAFTSMANSHIP was sought after in the earliest cars, and speed in the cars of the 1920s, then the 1930s was the era of styling. Beautiful body styling gave a car luxury appeal at a fraction of the cost of fine coachwork. A good design could be reproduced again and again on the production line. In the U.S., manufacturers such as Auburn, Cord, and Packard all made magnificent-looking cars in the 1930s – vast, extravagant cars that Hollywood stars posed beside, and Chicago gangsters drove. Such cars were not always well built, but with huge engines and elegant bodywork, they were usually fast and always glamorous.

Distinctive "V" front for sporty look

Elegant boat-shaped tail – with no trunklid

HEADING FOR THE SUN
The Depression years of the 1930s may have been hard for the poor, but for the rich and famous they were the golden days of grand touring, or *grand routier*. Nothing followed a round of parties in Paris more naturally than a leisurely drive south to the French Riviera in a sleek open tourer like one of these Peugeots.

Entire metal tail section made in single pressing

Auburn insignia

CAR FOR A STAR
You had to be someone special to be seen in a car like this. For a two-seater with minimal luggage space, it was massive – over 17 ft (almost 6 m) long, very tall and wide and clearly designed to impress. Film star Marlene Dietrich drove one.

Impractical but stylish whitewall tires

ESSENTIAL EQUIPMENT
The Auburn came complete with a locker for golf clubs and a radio as standard. The roof folded neatly down under the metal flap behind the passengers.

Golf-club hatch

Radio aerial

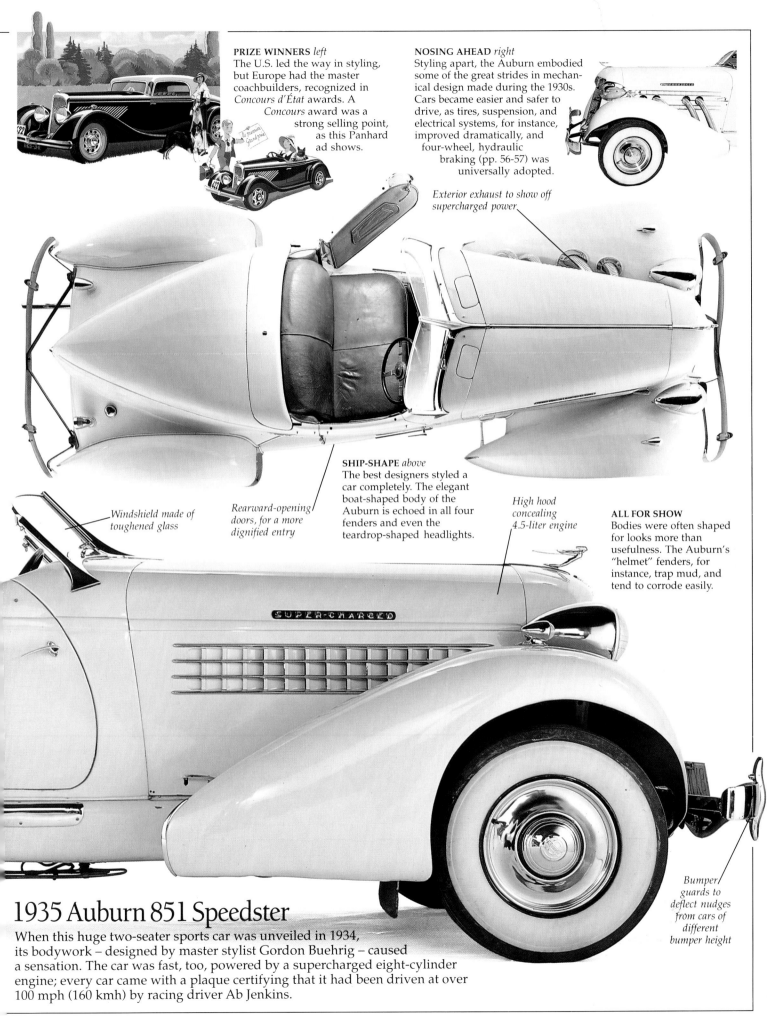

PRIZE WINNERS *left*
The U.S. led the way in styling, but Europe had the master coachbuilders, recognized in *Concours d'État* awards. A *Concours* award was a strong selling point, as this Panhard ad shows.

NOSING AHEAD *right*
Styling apart, the Auburn embodied some of the great strides in mechanical design made during the 1930s. Cars became easier and safer to drive, as tires, suspension, and electrical systems, for instance, improved dramatically, and four-wheel, hydraulic braking (pp. 56-57) was universally adopted.

Exterior exhaust to show off supercharged power

Windshield made of toughened glass

Rearward-opening doors, for a more dignified entry

SHIP-SHAPE *above*
The best designers styled a car completely. The elegant boat-shaped body of the Auburn is echoed in all four fenders and even the teardrop-shaped headlights.

High hood concealing 4.5-liter engine

ALL FOR SHOW
Bodies were often shaped for looks more than usefulness. The Auburn's "helmet" fenders, for instance, trap mud, and tend to corrode easily.

Bumper guards to deflect nudges from cars of different bumper height

1935 Auburn 851 Speedster

When this huge two-seater sports car was unveiled in 1934, its bodywork – designed by master stylist Gordon Buehrig – caused a sensation. The car was fast, too, powered by a supercharged eight-cylinder engine; every car came with a plaque certifying that it had been driven at over 100 mph (160 kmh) by racing driver Ab Jenkins.

Family motoring

I**N THE UNITED STATES, MANY MILLIONS OF PEOPLE** had already bought their own cars by 1930 – even though some may have had to sell their best furniture or mortgage their homes to pay for one. In the rest of the world, the price of a car was still beyond all but the wealthy.

Gradually, though, prices came down, and more and more middle-class families bought their first cars. The cars they bought were modest, inexpensive little sedans like the Austin Ten, the Opel Kadett, and the Ford Y. With small engines and upright bodywork, they offered little in the way of performance. But roomy interiors provided enough space for both parents and children, and closed-in seats made them practical in all kinds of weather.

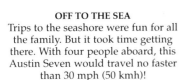

OFF TO THE SEA
Trips to the seashore were fun for all the family. But it took time getting there. With four people aboard, this Austin Seven would travel no faster than 30 mph (50 kmh)!

MOMMY! CAN WE HAVE A CAR?
Carmakers aimed their cars, and their ads, squarely at the family. How many parents, burdened with babies and luggage, must have succumbed to this temptation to buy the Ford Y?

PLAY ROOM
Family cars of the 1930s were designed for maximum passenger space. The rear doors of the Austin Ten open backward for easy access, and the back seat extends well over the rear wheels.

Windshield opens for cool air in summer

Drum brakes on all four wheels

Lightweight wire wheels

1936 Austin Ten
With its modest performance, practical design, and low selling price, the Austin Ten is typical of the family cars of the 1930s. It is actually a bigger, more refined version of the famous "baby" Austin Seven, the first popular British car.

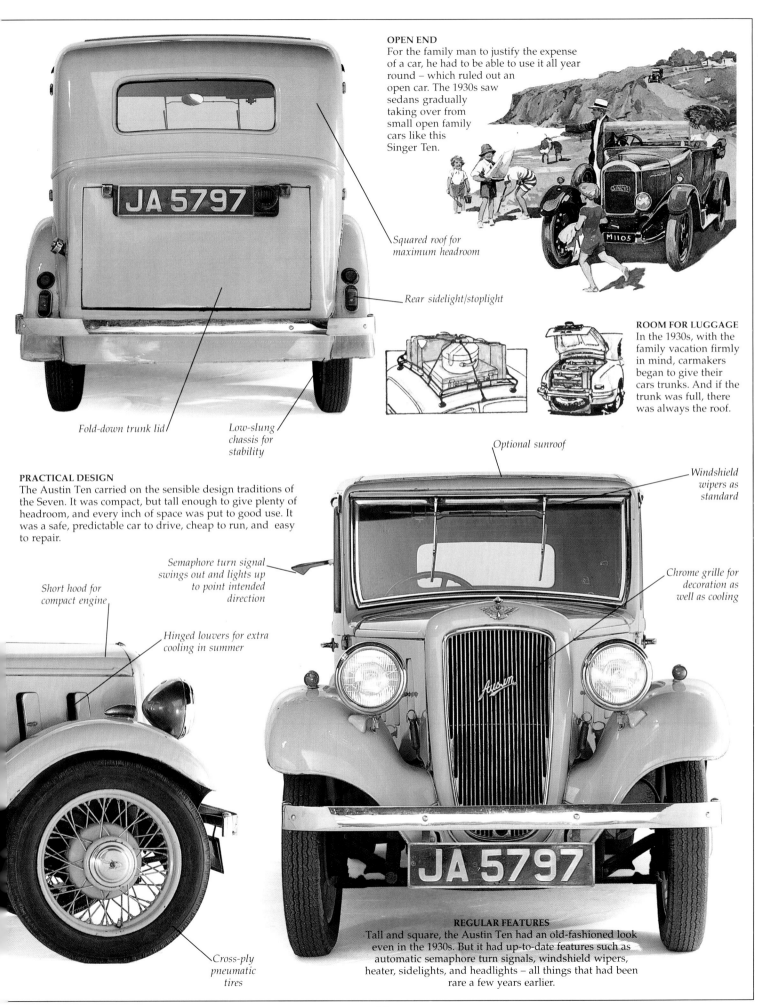

OPEN END
For the family man to justify the expense of a car, he had to be able to use it all year round – which ruled out an open car. The 1930s saw sedans gradually taking over from small open family cars like this Singer Ten.

Squared roof for maximum headroom

Rear sidelight/stoplight

JA 5797

Fold-down trunk lid

Low-slung chassis for stability

ROOM FOR LUGGAGE
In the 1930s, with the family vacation firmly in mind, carmakers began to give their cars trunks. And if the trunk was full, there was always the roof.

Optional sunroof

Windshield wipers as standard

PRACTICAL DESIGN
The Austin Ten carried on the sensible design traditions of the Seven. It was compact, but tall enough to give plenty of headroom, and every inch of space was put to good use. It was a safe, predictable car to drive, cheap to run, and easy to repair.

Semaphore turn signal swings out and lights up to point intended direction

Short hood for compact engine

Hinged louvers for extra cooling in summer

Chrome grille for decoration as well as cooling

JA 5797

Cross-ply pneumatic tires

REGULAR FEATURES
Tall and square, the Austin Ten had an old-fashioned look even in the 1930s. But it had up-to-date features such as automatic semaphore turn signals, windshield wipers, heater, sidelights, and headlights – all things that had been rare a few years earlier.

High performance

THE 1950s SAW THE CREATION of a series of remarkable high-performance cars. With the gasoline rationing of World War II ending in 1950, designers started working on cars that moved faster than ever. Racing cars had been capable of speeds of over 140 mph (220 kmh) before the war, but most road cars were much slower. In the early 1950s, however, a number of expensive 140 mph sports cars emerged from the factories of big companies like Jaguar and Mercedes-Benz and specialists such as Porsche, Aston Martin, Maserati, and Ferrari. Designed with both road and track in mind, they were often called Grand Tourers, or GTs. But the GTs of the 1950s were very different from the big open Grand Tourers of the 1920s and 1930s. The new GTs cars were compact, usually closed-in, two-seaters – cars not for leisurely motoring to the shore, but for screeching around winding roads at terrifying speeds. Many were winners on the racetrack, and could often match these performances on the road. Indeed, the road version of the Mercedes-Benz 300SL was one-third more powerful than the racing prototype.

ROAD RACE
The famous Mille Miglia (1,000 Miles) was an endurance race for road cars run over 1,000 miles of winding public roads in Italy. The 300SL excelled several times in the race and, in 1955, won outright.

SPACE FRAME *below*
Designers of GTs sought to keep weight to a minimum. Mercedes succeeded by making the 300SL's unique chassis from tubular steel. The frame was light and strong – but its high sides were the reason for the "gullwing" doors.

1957 Mercedes-Benz 300SL "Gullwing"

With futuristic bodywork matched by advanced engineering that gave the car 144 mph (230 kmh) performance, the Mercedes-Benz 300SL was a true classic.

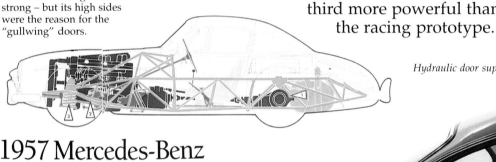

Hydraulic door supports

Stylized mudguard remnant

Quick-release "knock-off" wheel lock

Red-leather-lined passenger compartment

High sill because of tube chassis

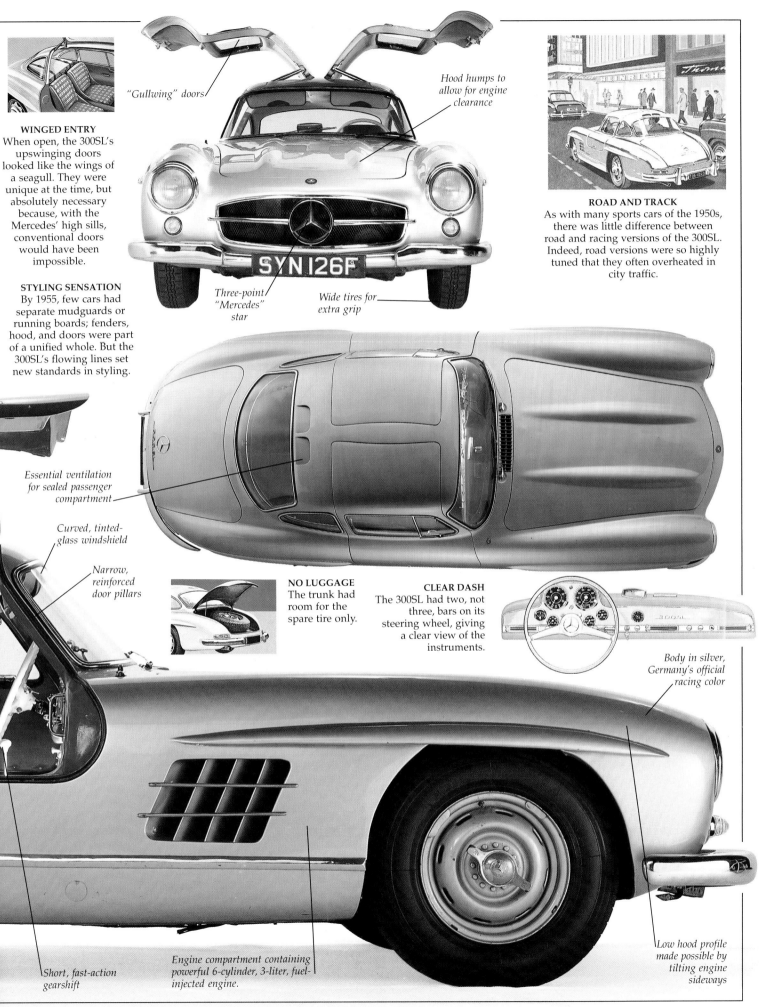

WINGED ENTRY
When open, the 300SL's upswinging doors looked like the wings of a seagull. They were unique at the time, but absolutely necessary because, with the Mercedes' high sills, conventional doors would have been impossible.

STYLING SENSATION
By 1955, few cars had separate mudguards or running boards; fenders, hood, and doors were part of a unified whole. But the 300SL's flowing lines set new standards in styling.

"Gullwing" doors

Hood humps to allow for engine clearance

ROAD AND TRACK
As with many sports cars of the 1950s, there was little difference between road and racing versions of the 300SL. Indeed, road versions were so highly tuned that they often overheated in city traffic.

Three-point "Mercedes" star

Wide tires for extra grip

Essential ventilation for sealed passenger compartment

Curved, tinted-glass windshield

Narrow, reinforced door pillars

NO LUGGAGE
The trunk had room for the spare tire only.

CLEAR DASH
The 300SL had two, not three, bars on its steering wheel, giving a clear view of the instruments.

Body in silver, Germany's official racing color

Short, fast-action gearshift

Engine compartment containing powerful 6-cylinder, 3-liter, fuel-injected engine.

Low hood profile made possible by tilting engine sideways

American dream

Every period in the history of the automobile is remembered for its own particular style or technological trend. But perhaps none was quite so distinctive as the mid-1950s to mid-1960s in the U.S. This was the era of rock'n'roll and drive-in movies, fast food and new freeways. The booming confidence of America in those years was reflected in some of the most outrageous, flashiest cars ever made. Competition among American carmakers was fierce, and each tried to outdo the others in the glamour of its cars. Constant demand for a new sensation tested the skills of designers such as Harley Earl and Bill Mitchell to the limits. Expanses of chrome and fin were matched by all kinds of technological gimmicks. Though the styling was excessive, innovations such as wraparound windshields and power steering were genuine and lasting.

Cadillac motif

FIN TIME
Nothing is more characteristic of American styling in the 1950s than the fin. Strictly for show, fins first appeared in 1955 and got bigger and bigger until the end of the 1950s. They finally disappeared in the mid-1970s.

BEAUTIFUL OR UGLY?
Unlike cars today, which change little in looks from year to year, new models appeared almost every year in the United States in the 1950s and 1960s. This picture shows the 1959 Fords. Believe it or not, they were advertised as "The World's Most Beautifully Proportioned Cars."

Massive chromed bumper

Concealed exhaust pipe

BIG AND SMALL
American cars of the 1950s were small inside considering their vast proportions. Space was sacrificed for the sake of styling. Trunks were often very shallow – which is why the Ford made use of the back-seat space (left).

Stylized "finned" hub cap

Decorative white tire ring

28

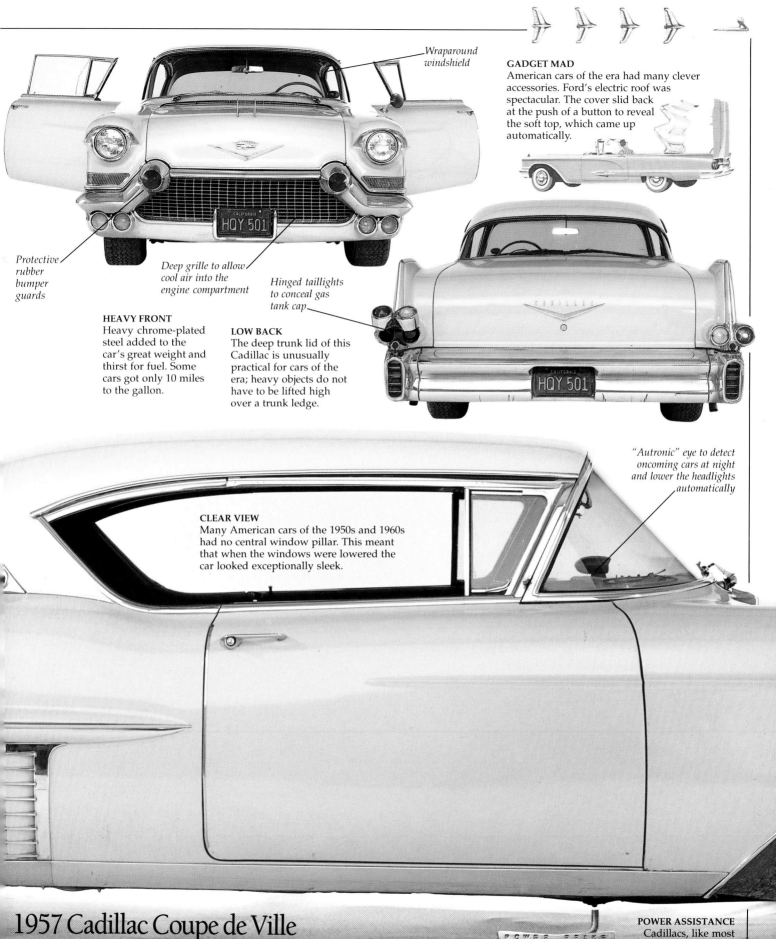

Wraparound windshield

Protective rubber bumper guards

Deep grille to allow cool air into the engine compartment

GADGET MAD
American cars of the era had many clever accessories. Ford's electric roof was spectacular. The cover slid back at the push of a button to reveal the soft top, which came up automatically.

HEAVY FRONT
Heavy chrome-plated steel added to the car's great weight and thirst for fuel. Some cars got only 10 miles to the gallon.

LOW BACK
The deep trunk lid of this Cadillac is unusually practical for cars of the era; heavy objects do not have to be lifted high over a trunk ledge.

Hinged taillights to conceal gas tank cap

"Autronic" eye to detect oncoming cars at night and lower the headlights automatically

CLEAR VIEW
Many American cars of the 1950s and 1960s had no central window pillar. This meant that when the windows were lowered the car looked exceptionally sleek.

1957 Cadillac Coupe de Ville

Typical of American cars of the 1950s, the Coupe de Ville is almost 18 ft (6 m) long and extravagantly finned and chromed. It also has many advanced technical features, such as electrically powered windows and reclining seats, and a smooth eight-cylinder engine.

POWER ASSISTANCE
Cadillacs, like most American luxury cars of the time, had "power-assisted" steering and braking – essential in such heavy cars.

Cars for the city

LITTLE MOUSE
The cheap and cheerful Fiat 500 "Topolino" (Little Mouse) became Italy's most popular car.

In the 1950s, small cars were cheaper than ever before. Cars such as the Volkswagen Beetle and the Renault 4 were so basic and inexpensive that they sold by the million. Indeed, so many cars were sold that city roads began to clog up. In London, the number of cars doubled; in Paris, *zones bleues* were imposed to restrict traffic; and in New York, massive urban freeways were built to relieve congestion. No wonder, then, that tiny "bubble" cars, such as the Italian Isetta, soon became all the rage – even though they were built essentially for economy rather than compactness. For a family, though, they were just a bit too small. One answer was the Mini, launched in 1959. A full-scale car in a tiny package, the Mini was revolutionary. To make room for four adults in such a small car, engine and transmission had to take up as little space as possible. So designer Alec Issigonis set the engine transversely (across the car), driving the front wheels. The idea worked so well that now nearly all family cars have the same layout.

ITALIAN MINI
The tiny Fiat 500, launched in 1957, was even smaller than the Mini and sold almost as well. But passengers were cramped and the rear-engine layout proved a dead end.

BUBBLING OVER
For a few years in the 1950s, tiny "bubble" cars like this Isetta were popular with city-dwellers. They could seat two, and had 3 wheels and a tiny 2-cylinder engine in the back. They were short enough to be parked headfirst – which is just as well, because the door was at the front.

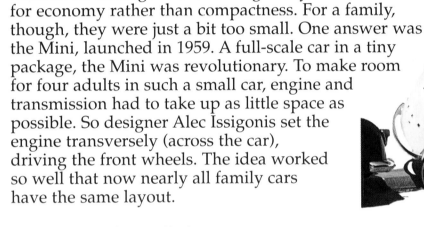

HIGH COMPRESSION
Fitting everything under the Mini's compact hood was a remarkable feat. Squeezed into the tiny hood are all the engine components, cooling system, transmission, steering gear, and the entire front suspension.

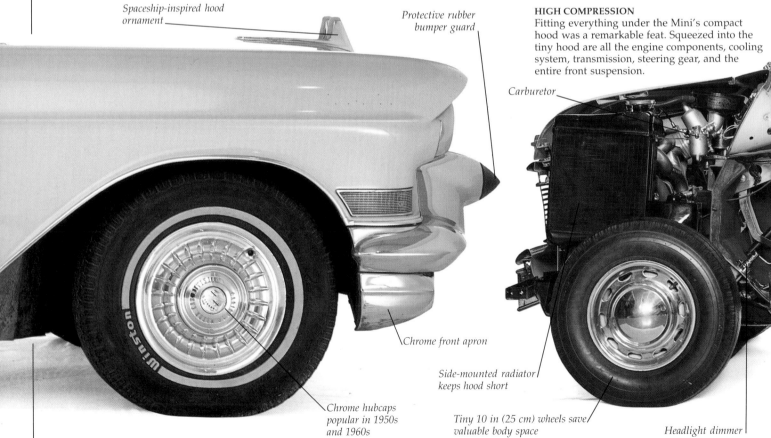

Spaceship-inspired hood ornament

Protective rubber bumper guard

Carburetor

Chrome front apron

Side-mounted radiator keeps hood short

Chrome hubcaps popular in 1950s and 1960s

Tiny 10 in (25 cm) wheels save valuable body space

Headlight dimmer

CITY CAR
Designers are still toying with the idea of the city car – a tiny, economical car ideal for parking and driving short distances. Many designs are electrically powered; this Ligier from France uses a 1-cylinder gasoline engine.

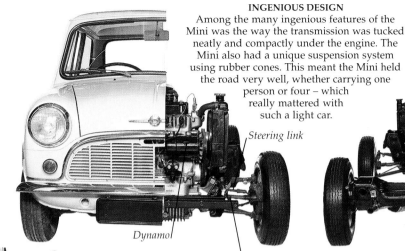

INGENIOUS DESIGN
Among the many ingenious features of the Mini was the way the transmission was tucked neatly and compactly under the engine. The Mini also had a unique suspension system using rubber cones. This meant the Mini held the road very well, whether carrying one person or four – which really mattered with such a light car.

Steering link

Dynamo

Drive shaft

Rear subframe

ROOM FOR THE FAMILY
The Mini's capacity for luggage and people was always its selling point. People competed to see just what could be squeezed inside. Once, in 1972, 46 students of Queensland University, Australia, crammed in!

SPACE-SAVING
To gain luggage space, the Mini did away with dashboard, trim panels, window winders – even door handles.

SITTING ROOM
An overhead view shows how the Mini succeeded in keeping the engine compact and providing space for four passengers and luggage. This priority for passengers has been the Mini's lasting legacy; few car buyers would now settle for less space.

CHARGE FROM BEHIND
To save valuable space under the hood, the Mini's battery is concealed in its own compartment under the trunk floor, along with the spare tire.

Sliding windows

Rearview mirror

Spare tire

Starter button

Hand brake

Simple door pull

Deep door pocket

Soundproofing felt underlay

Extra luggage space beneath rear seat

1959 Morris Mini Minor

A masterpiece of design, the Mini was a milestone in the history of the car. With its extraordinary compactness, economy, and performance, it set a precedent followed by all but a few small cars today.

Racing car

FORMULA ONE RACING CARS are the ultimate speed machines, worlds apart from everyday road cars. Their open, one-seater bodies are made of new ultralight materials and are so low-slung they almost scrape the ground. The "fuselage" and wings are aerodynamically shaped to keep the wheels firmly on the road. Huge, wide tires give extra traction at high speeds. And enormously powerful engines propel them around the track at speeds in excess of 190 mph (300kph). Auto racing is so fiercely competitive that designers are always trying new ideas to give their cars the edge in performance. But each car has to comply with strict rules laid down for Formula One cars, covering everything from the size of the fuel tank to the shape of the floor pan. To keep up with new developments, the rules must be updated almost every season, and the ingenuity of designers is tested to its limits as they try to adapt their designs to the new rules – and still beat their rivals.

FINISHING SCHOOL
The 500 cc events that started in the 1950s have proved an ideal way into racing for many a budding Grand Prix driver.

ONE FOR THE ROAD
Prewar racers looked little different from road cars.

DOUBLING UP
In the days before "slicks," cars were often fitted with double rear wheels for extra traction in the hill-climb events popular until the mid-1950s.

AIR PRESSURE
Racing-car bodies are not only streamlined to lessen air resistance, they are also shaped so that the air flowing over the car helps keep it on the road. The front and rear wings act like upside-down airplane wings to push the wheels onto the ground.

GROUND EFFECT
In 1979, many racing cars had "skirts" almost touching the ground – so that, at high speed, air rushing under the car sucked it closer to the ground. This "ground effect" improved road-holding so much that skirts were soon banned because drivers were going too fast. Now cars have a "waist" to give the same effect.

Front coil springs and shocks mounted inboard to cut air resistance

Roll bar to protect driver's head in a crash

Rearview mirror

Sponsor's logo – Formula One racing is now such an expensive business that sponsorship is vital

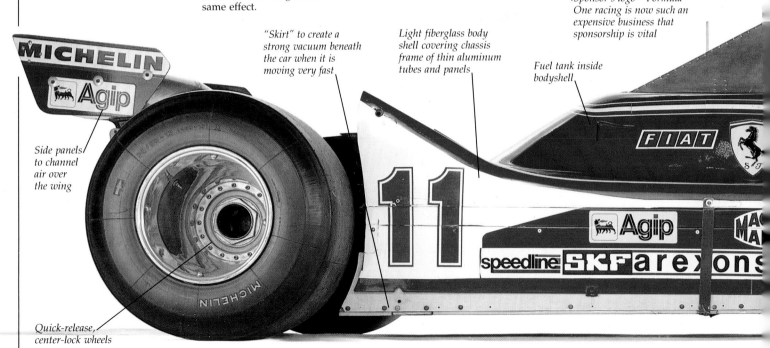

"Skirt" to create a strong vacuum beneath the car when it is moving very fast

Light fiberglass body shell covering chassis frame of thin aluminum tubes and panels

Fuel tank inside bodyshell

Side panels to channel air over the wing

Quick-release, center-lock wheels

1979 Ferrari 312 T4

One of the most successful modern Grand Prix cars, the Ferrari 312 took first Niki Lauda and then, in 1979, Jody Scheckter to the world drivers' championship.

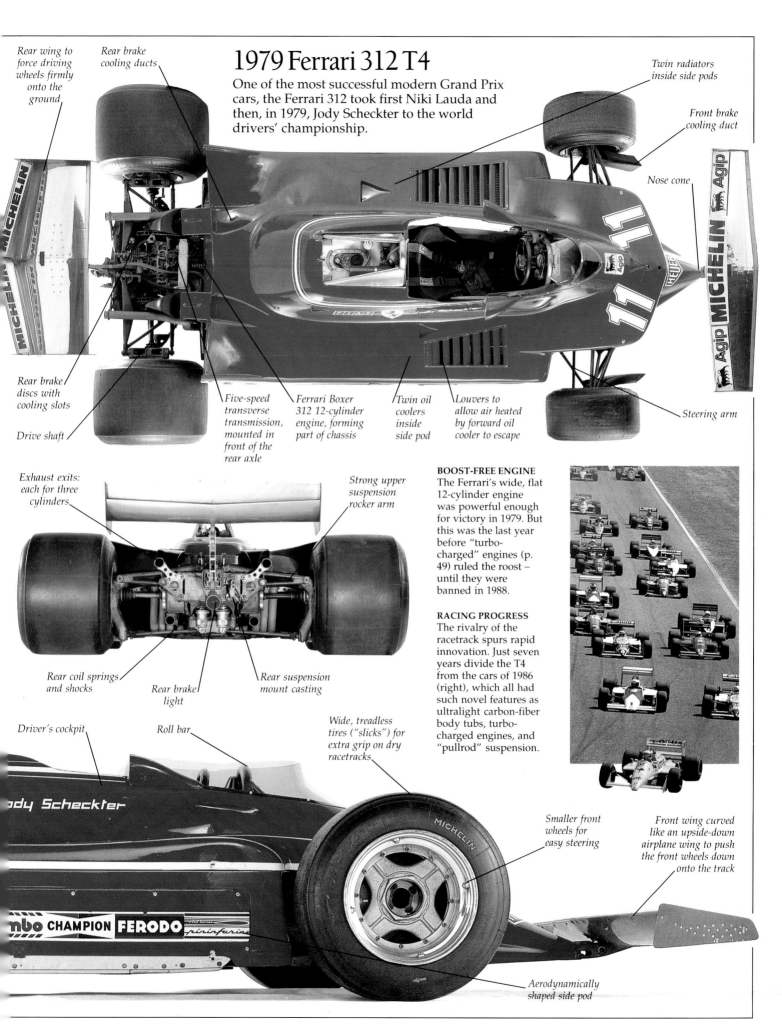

Rear wing to force driving wheels firmly onto the ground

Rear brake cooling ducts

Twin radiators inside side pods

Front brake cooling duct

Nose cone

Rear brake discs with cooling slots

Drive shaft

Five-speed transverse transmission, mounted in front of the rear axle

Ferrari Boxer 312 12-cylinder engine, forming part of chassis

Twin oil coolers inside side pod

Louvers to allow air heated by forward oil cooler to escape

Steering arm

Exhaust exits: each for three cylinders

Strong upper suspension rocker arm

Rear coil springs and shocks

Rear brake light

Rear suspension mount casting

BOOST-FREE ENGINE
The Ferrari's wide, flat 12-cylinder engine was powerful enough for victory in 1979. But this was the last year before "turbo-charged" engines (p. 49) ruled the roost – until they were banned in 1988.

RACING PROGRESS
The rivalry of the racetrack spurs rapid innovation. Just seven years divide the T4 from the cars of 1986 (right), which all had such novel features as ultralight carbon-fiber body tubs, turbo-charged engines, and "pullrod" suspension.

Driver's cockpit

Roll bar

Wide, treadless tires ("slicks") for extra grip on dry racetracks

Smaller front wheels for easy steering

Front wing curved like an upside-down airplane wing to push the front wheels down onto the track

Aerodynamically shaped side pod

Creating a car

CREATING A NEW CAR is a costly business, involving hundreds of people and years of intensive research. So a carmaker has to be confident that the car is going to sell before developing the concept far. Even before the designer draws the first rough sketch for the new car, the maker's requirements are laid down in detail in a "design brief" – including the car's precise dimensions, how many passengers it will carry, how many doors it will have, the engine layout and the transmission, and much more. The route from the initial sketch to the finished car is a long one, and the design is subject to close scrutiny at all stages in the process. Several full-scale models are built – first usually from clay, then from fiber glass – and the design is constantly modified and refined. By the time the first production version rolls out of the factory, the car will work (and sell) perfectly – or so the carmaker hopes!

FIRST SKETCH
Nearly every new car starts as a sketch on the designer's drawing board. The designer may draw dozens of these sketches before everyone is happy enough to proceed to a more detailed design drawing, or "rendering."

ARCHITECT'S CAR
Designs that are too unconventional or impractical tend to be abandoned at an early stage – such as this design for a cheap city car proposed in the 1920s by the famous modern architect Le Corbusier.

The interior is left blank since this mock-up is intended to show only the body styling

The clay is laid over a roughly shaped framework, or "armature," of wood and foam slightly smaller than the finished model

Full-size clay model

For the Fiat Panda, the designers were asked to come up with a car that was light, roomy, economical and practical. After numerous design drawings and renderings, they built this full-scale model of the body shell for their proposed car. It differs only in minor details from the real thing.

COMPUTER POWER
Computers are playing an increasingly important part in the design process. Most manufacturers now use Computer Aided Design (CAD) techniques, at least once the basic shape has been decided upon. Often a clay model of the design is scanned (right) to set up the computer with a complete set of profiles and contours (left). The computer can then be used to analyze such things as stresses in the body panel and to change the design at the touch of a button.

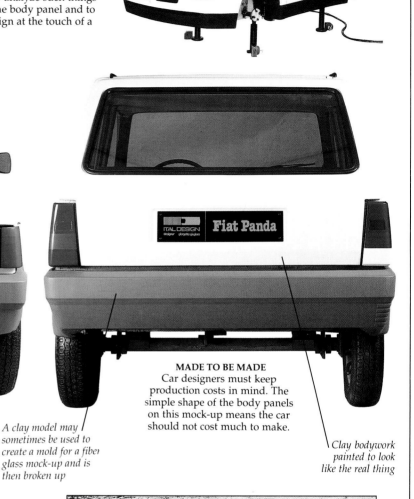

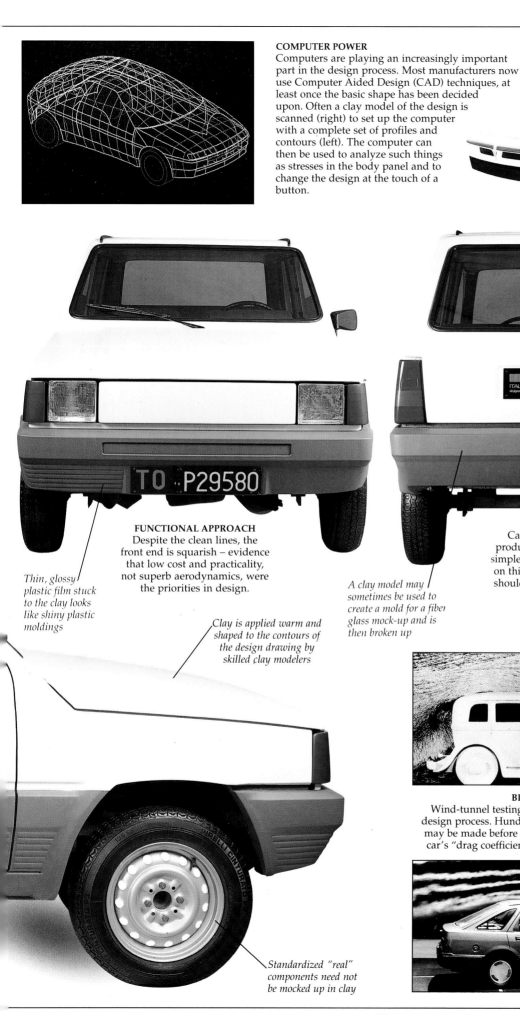

FUNCTIONAL APPROACH
Despite the clean lines, the front end is squarish – evidence that low cost and practicality, not superb aerodynamics, were the priorities in design.

Thin, glossy plastic film stuck to the clay looks like shiny plastic moldings

Clay is applied warm and shaped to the contours of the design drawing by skilled clay modelers

A clay model may sometimes be used to create a mold for a fiber glass mock-up and is then broken up

MADE TO BE MADE
Car designers must keep production costs in mind. The simple shape of the body panels on this mock-up means the car should not cost much to make.

Clay bodywork painted to look like the real thing

Standardized "real" components need not be mocked up in clay

BLOWING IN THE WIND
Wind-tunnel testing has long been an important part of the design process. Hundreds of minor changes to the body profile may be made before the designers are finally satisfied that the car's "drag coefficient" is as low as they can practically get it.

The anatomy of a car

THE DAYS WHEN EVERY CAR had a strong chassis and a separate coach-built body are long gone. Almost all cars today are of "unit" construction, which means that chassis and body are made as a single unit – although some may also have a small "subframe" like the car here. Unit construction makes a car both light and strong. It is also perfect for mass production since it involves little more than welding together steel sheets stamped into shape by machines – all of which can be done by robots on the production line.

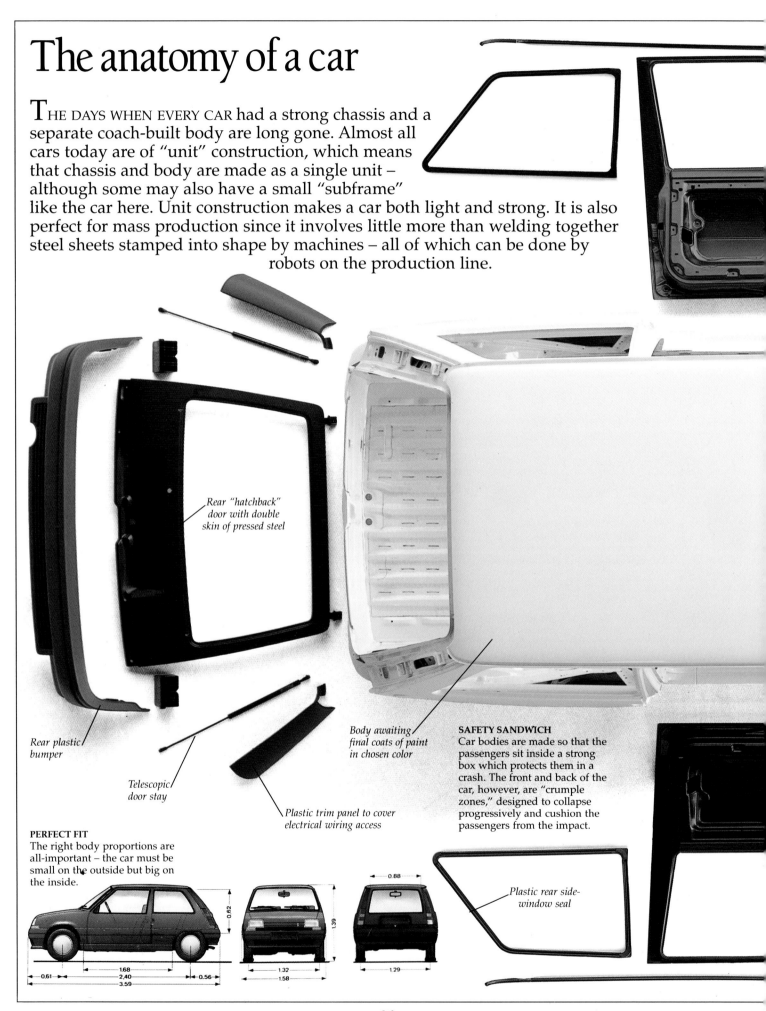

Rear "hatchback" door with double skin of pressed steel

Rear plastic bumper

Telescopic door stay

Plastic trim panel to cover electrical wiring access

Body awaiting final coats of paint in chosen color

SAFETY SANDWICH
Car bodies are made so that the passengers sit inside a strong box which protects them in a crash. The front and back of the car, however, are "crumple zones," designed to collapse progressively and cushion the passengers from the impact.

PERFECT FIT
The right body proportions are all-important – the car must be small on the outside but big on the inside.

Plastic rear side-window seal

0.88

0.62

1.39

1.68
2.40
3.59
0.61
0.56

1.32
1.58

1.29

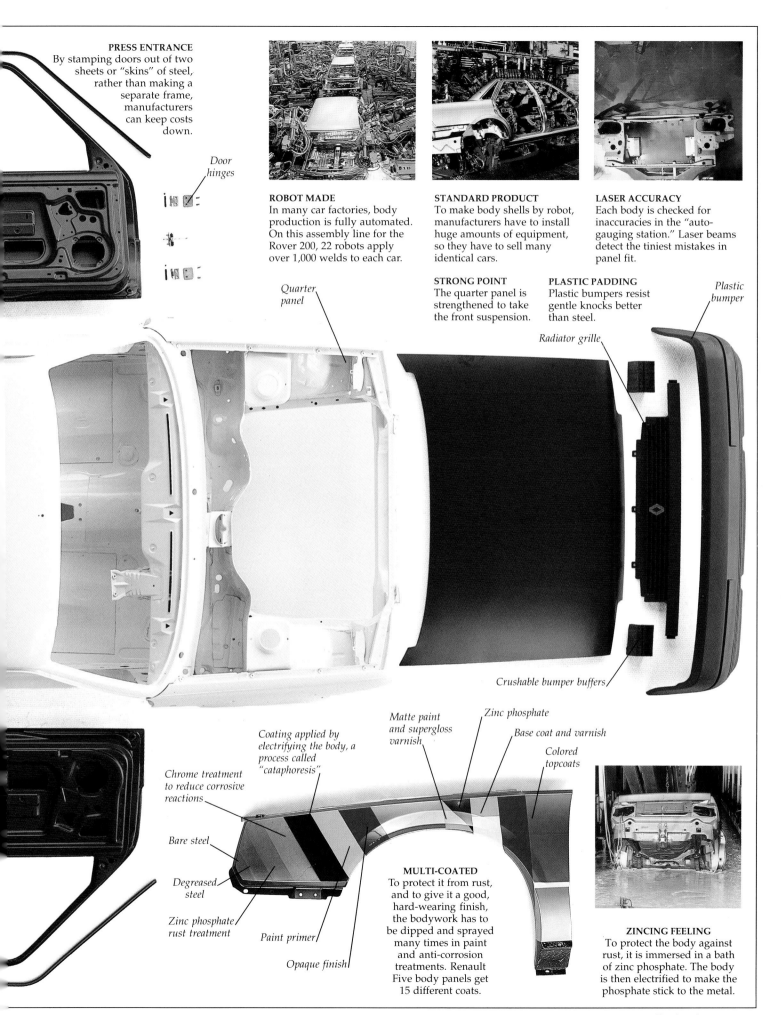

PRESS ENTRANCE
By stamping doors out of two sheets or "skins" of steel, rather than making a separate frame, manufacturers can keep costs down.

Door hinges

ROBOT MADE
In many car factories, body production is fully automated. On this assembly line for the Rover 200, 22 robots apply over 1,000 welds to each car.

STANDARD PRODUCT
To make body shells by robot, manufacturers have to install huge amounts of equipment, so they have to sell many identical cars.

LASER ACCURACY
Each body is checked for inaccuracies in the "auto-gauging station." Laser beams detect the tiniest mistakes in panel fit.

STRONG POINT
The quarter panel is strengthened to take the front suspension.

PLASTIC PADDING
Plastic bumpers resist gentle knocks better than steel.

Quarter panel

Plastic bumper

Radiator grille

Crushable bumper buffers

Matte paint and supergloss varnish

Zinc phosphate

Base coat and varnish

Colored topcoats

Coating applied by electrifying the body, a process called "cataphoresis"

Chrome treatment to reduce corrosive reactions

Bare steel

Degreased steel

Zinc phosphate rust treatment

Paint primer

Opaque finish

MULTI-COATED
To protect it from rust, and to give it a good, hard-wearing finish, the bodywork has to be dipped and sprayed many times in paint and anti-corrosion treatments. Renault Five body panels get 15 different coats.

ZINCING FEELING
To protect the body against rust, it is immersed in a bath of zinc phosphate. The body is then electrified to make the phosphate stick to the metal.

Continued on next page

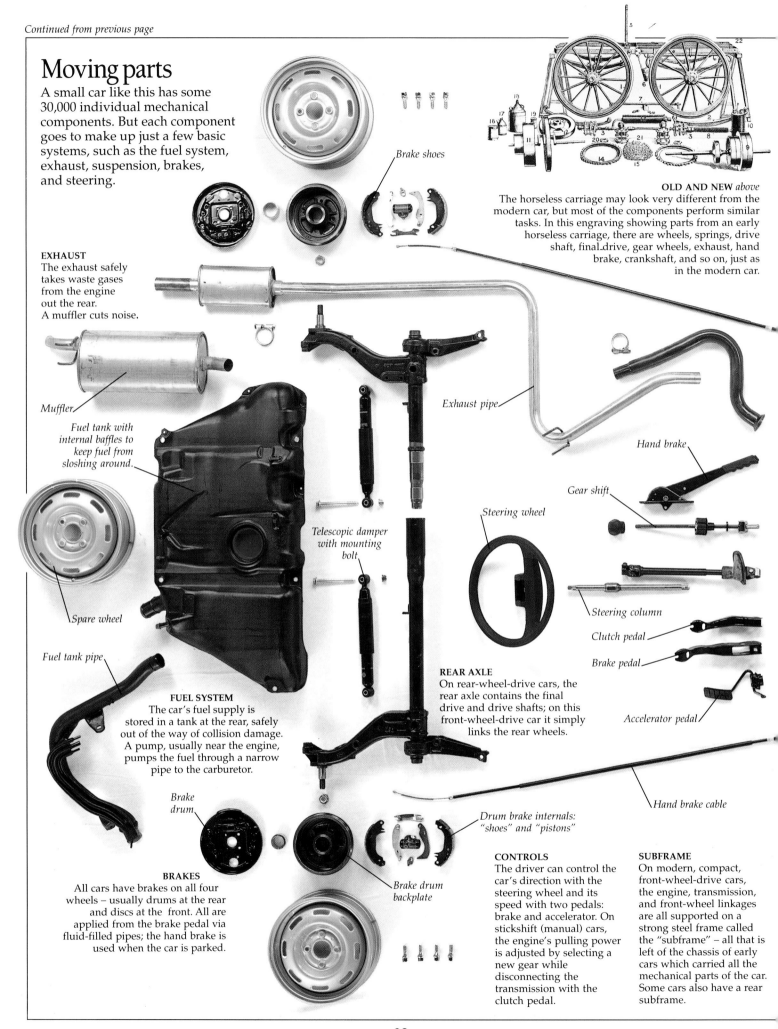

Continued from previous page

Moving parts

A small car like this has some 30,000 individual mechanical components. But each component goes to make up just a few basic systems, such as the fuel system, exhaust, suspension, brakes, and steering.

Brake shoes

OLD AND NEW *above*
The horseless carriage may look very different from the modern car, but most of the components perform similar tasks. In this engraving showing parts from an early horseless carriage, there are wheels, springs, drive shaft, final drive, gear wheels, exhaust, hand brake, crankshaft, and so on, just as in the modern car.

EXHAUST
The exhaust safely takes waste gases from the engine out the rear. A muffler cuts noise.

Exhaust pipe

Muffler

Hand brake

Fuel tank with internal baffles to keep fuel from sloshing around.

Gear shift

Steering wheel

Telescopic damper with mounting bolt

Steering column

Clutch pedal

Brake pedal

Spare wheel

REAR AXLE
On rear-wheel-drive cars, the rear axle contains the final drive and drive shafts; on this front-wheel-drive car it simply links the rear wheels.

Accelerator pedal

Fuel tank pipe

FUEL SYSTEM
The car's fuel supply is stored in a tank at the rear, safely out of the way of collision damage. A pump, usually near the engine, pumps the fuel through a narrow pipe to the carburetor.

Brake drum

Hand brake cable

Drum brake internals: "shoes" and "pistons"

Brake drum backplate

BRAKES
All cars have brakes on all four wheels – usually drums at the rear and discs at the front. All are applied from the brake pedal via fluid-filled pipes; the hand brake is used when the car is parked.

CONTROLS
The driver can control the car's direction with the steering wheel and its speed with two pedals: brake and accelerator. On stickshift (manual) cars, the engine's pulling power is adjusted by selecting a new gear while disconnecting the transmission with the clutch pedal.

SUBFRAME
On modern, compact, front-wheel-drive cars, the engine, transmission, and front-wheel linkages are all supported on a strong steel frame called the "subframe" – all that is left of the chassis of early cars which carried all the mechanical parts of the car. Some cars also have a rear subframe.

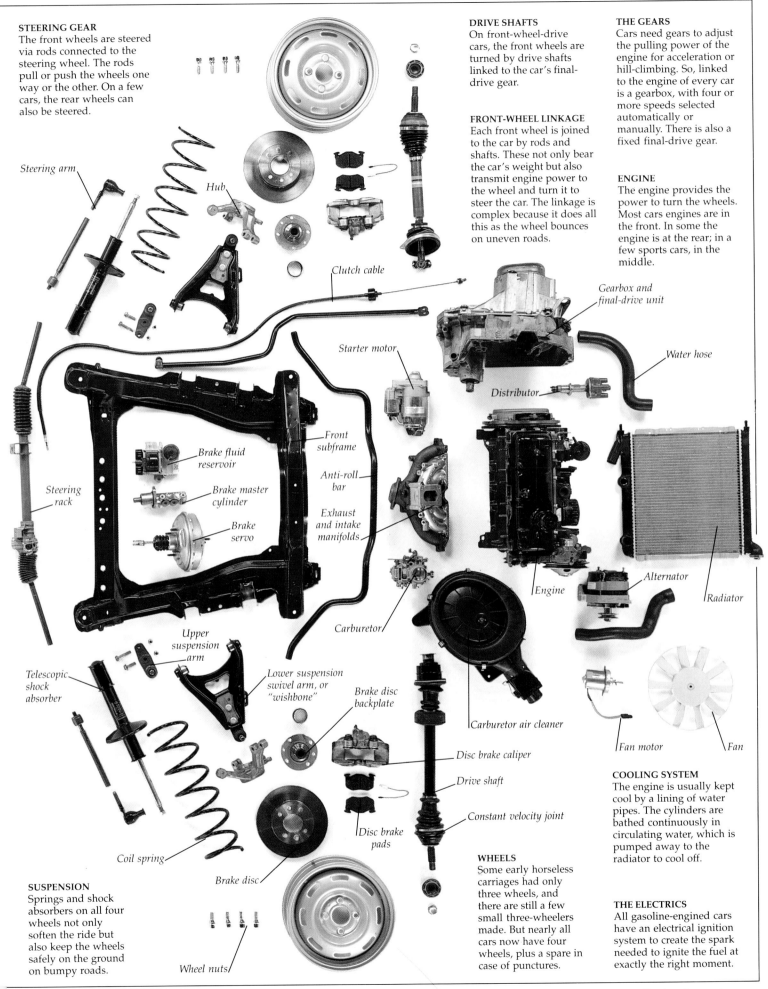

STEERING GEAR
The front wheels are steered via rods connected to the steering wheel. The rods pull or push the wheels one way or the other. On a few cars, the rear wheels can also be steered.

Steering arm

Hub

Steering rack

Brake fluid reservoir

Brake master cylinder

Brake servo

Front subframe

Anti-roll bar

Exhaust and intake manifolds

Upper suspension arm

Telescopic shock absorber

Lower suspension swivel arm, or "wishbone"

Carburetor

Brake disc backplate

Coil spring

SUSPENSION
Springs and shock absorbers on all four wheels not only soften the ride but also keep the wheels safely on the ground on bumpy roads.

Wheel nuts

Brake disc

Disc brake caliper

Disc brake pads

Clutch cable

Starter motor

Carburetor air cleaner

Drive shaft

Constant velocity joint

WHEELS
Some early horseless carriages had only three wheels, and there are still a few small three-wheelers made. But nearly all cars now have four wheels, plus a spare in case of punctures.

DRIVE SHAFTS
On front-wheel-drive cars, the front wheels are turned by drive shafts linked to the car's final-drive gear.

FRONT-WHEEL LINKAGE
Each front wheel is joined to the car by rods and shafts. These not only bear the car's weight but also transmit engine power to the wheel and turn it to steer the car. The linkage is complex because it does all this as the wheel bounces on uneven roads.

Gearbox and final-drive unit

Distributor

Engine

Alternator

THE GEARS
Cars need gears to adjust the pulling power of the engine for acceleration or hill-climbing. So, linked to the engine of every car is a gearbox, with four or more speeds selected automatically or manually. There is also a fixed final-drive gear.

ENGINE
The engine provides the power to turn the wheels. Most cars engines are in the front. In some the engine is at the rear; in a few sports cars, in the middle.

Water hose

Radiator

Fan motor

Fan

COOLING SYSTEM
The engine is usually kept cool by a lining of water pipes. The cylinders are bathed continuously in circulating water, which is pumped away to the radiator to cool off.

THE ELECTRICS
All gasoline-engined cars have an electrical ignition system to create the spark needed to ignite the fuel at exactly the right moment.

Continued on next page

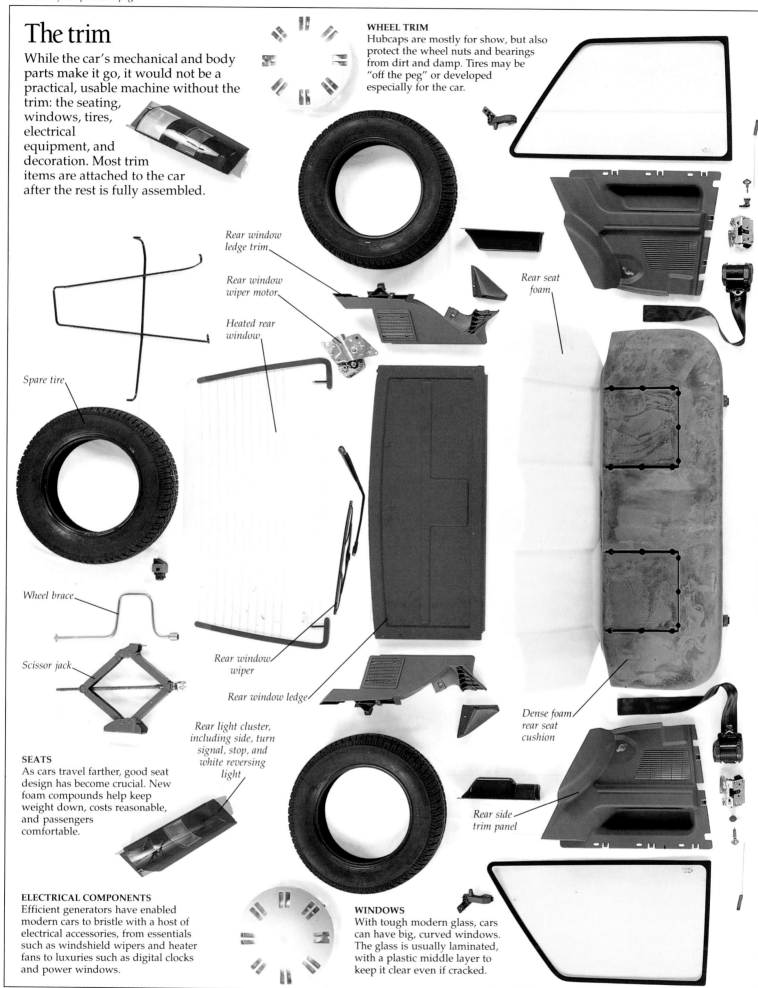

The trim

While the car's mechanical and body parts make it go, it would not be a practical, usable machine without the trim: the seating, windows, tires, electrical equipment, and decoration. Most trim items are attached to the car after the rest is fully assembled.

WHEEL TRIM
Hubcaps are mostly for show, but also protect the wheel nuts and bearings from dirt and damp. Tires may be "off the peg" or developed especially for the car.

Rear window ledge trim

Rear window wiper motor

Heated rear window

Rear seat foam

Spare tire

Wheel brace

Scissor jack

Rear window wiper

Rear window ledge

Dense foam rear seat cushion

Rear light cluster, including side, turn signal, stop, and white reversing light

Rear side trim panel

SEATS
As cars travel farther, good seat design has become crucial. New foam compounds help keep weight down, costs reasonable, and passengers comfortable.

ELECTRICAL COMPONENTS
Efficient generators have enabled modern cars to bristle with a host of electrical accessories, from essentials such as windshield wipers and heater fans to luxuries such as digital clocks and power windows.

WINDOWS
With tough modern glass, cars can have big, curved windows. The glass is usually laminated, with a plastic middle layer to keep it clear even if cracked.

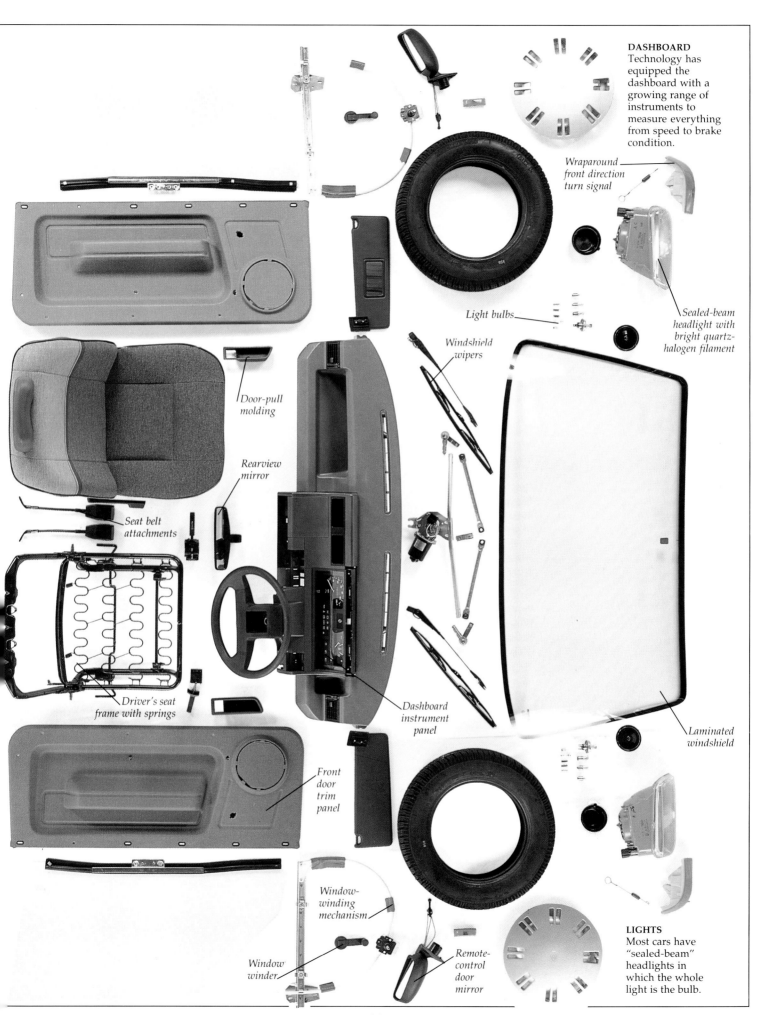

DASHBOARD Technology has equipped the dashboard with a growing range of instruments to measure everything from speed to brake condition.

Wraparound front direction turn signal

Sealed-beam headlight with bright quartz-halogen filament

Light bulbs

Windshield wipers

Door-pull molding

Rearview mirror

Seat belt attachments

Driver's seat frame with springs

Dashboard instrument panel

Laminated windshield

Front door trim panel

Window-winding mechanism

Window winder

Remote-control door mirror

LIGHTS Most cars have "sealed-beam" headlights in which the whole light is the bulb.

The driving force

THE POWERHOUSE under the hood of nearly every modern car is an internal combustion engine – just as it was in the first Benz well over a century ago. Today's engines are powerful, compact, and economical compared with their forerunners. They usually have four or more small cylinders and run fast, too – unlike the huge single- or twin-cylinder engines of the early days, which ticked over so slowly you could almost hear individual piston strokes. Yet the principles are still the same. The engine is a "combustion" engine because it "combusts" (burns) fuel, usually a mixture of gasoline and air. It is an "internal" combustion engine because the fuel burns inside the cylinders.

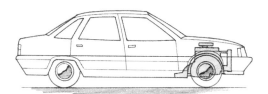

SMALL AND QUICK
Tucked away under the hood, modern car engines are compact, high revving, and powerful. This engine runs up to 6,000 rpm (revolutions per minute) and its four 500 cc cylinders push out 40 times as much power as the Benz below.

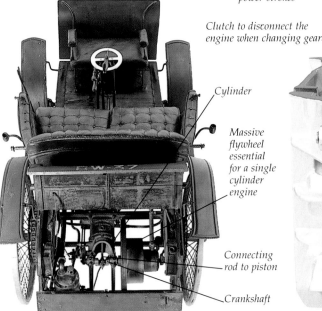

Cylinder

Massive flywheel essential for a single cylinder engine

Connecting rod to piston

Crankshaft

SLOW AND SIMPLE
The single big 1,140 cc cylinder of the 1898 Benz chugged around at a leisurely 1,200 rpm. All the workings of the engine are clearly exposed here: the connecting rod running up inside the cylinder, the crankshaft, the big flywheel, and so on.

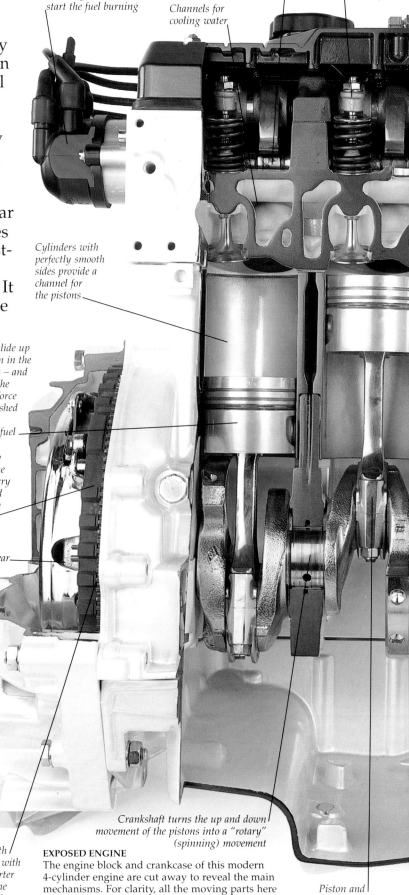

Distributor to send a spark to each cylinder at the right moment to start the fuel burning

Camshaft controls the opening and closing of the valves

Rocker arms to push the valves open

Channels for cooling water

Cylinders with perfectly smooth sides provide a channel for the pistons

Pistons slide up and down in the cylinders – and provide the driving force when pushed down by burning fuel

Flywheel of heavy steel to provide the momentum to carry the engine around smoothly between power strokes

Clutch to disconnect the engine when changing gear

Starter ring with teeth that mesh with teeth on the starter motor to spin the engine for starting

Crankshaft turns the up and down movement of the pistons into a "rotary" (spinning) movement

Piston and connecting rod turn the crankshaft

EXPOSED ENGINE
The engine block and crankcase of this modern 4-cylinder engine are cut away to reveal the main mechanisms. For clarity, all the moving parts here are chrome-plated and the block is enameled; in a complete engine, all the internals are bare metal.

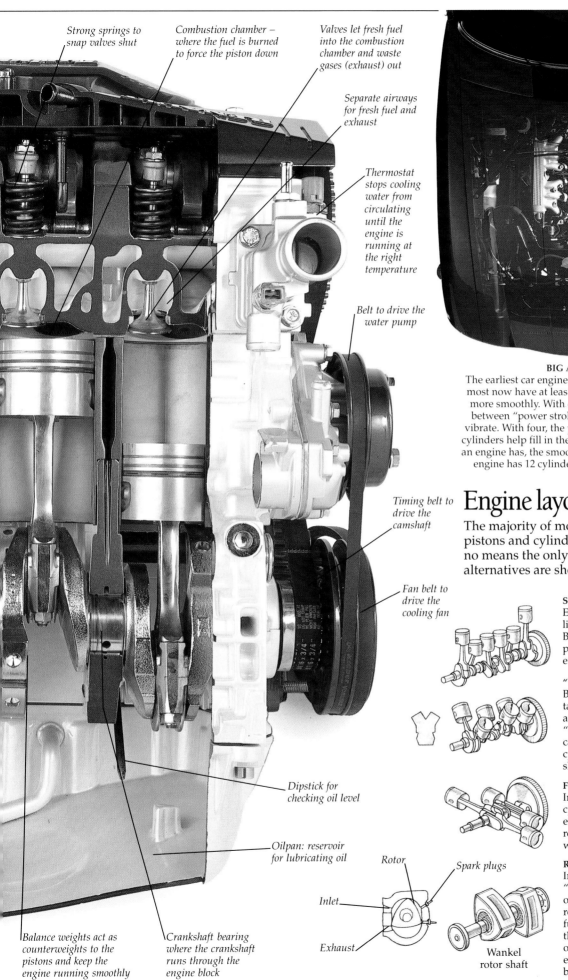

Strong springs to snap valves shut

Combustion chamber – where the fuel is burned to force the piston down

Valves let fresh fuel into the combustion chamber and waste gases (exhaust) out

Separate airways for fresh fuel and exhaust

Thermostat stops cooling water from circulating until the engine is running at the right temperature

Belt to drive the water pump

Timing belt to drive the camshaft

Fan belt to drive the cooling fan

Dipstick for checking oil level

Oilpan: reservoir for lubricating oil

Balance weights act as counterweights to the pistons and keep the engine running smoothly

Crankshaft bearing where the crankshaft runs through the engine block

BIG AND SMOOTH

The earliest car engines had only one or two cylinders; most now have at least four because a four runs much more smoothly. With one cylinder, there are big gaps between "power strokes" (p. 44), making the engine vibrate. With four, the power strokes on the other three cylinders help fill in the gaps. In fact, the more cylinders an engine has, the smoother it runs – this 5.3-liter Jaguar engine has 12 cylinders and is very smooth indeed.

Engine layouts

The majority of modern car engines have four pistons and cylinders set in line. Yet this is by no means the only possible arrangement. Some alternatives are shown below.

STRAIGHT SIX
Engines with six cylinders set in line are long, and costly to make. But they can be very smooth and powerful and are popular for large, expensive sedans.

"V" SIX
Big straight engines are too long and tall to fit into low-slung sports cars, and their long crankshafts can "whip" under stress. So many sports cars have compact "V" engines with cylinders interlocking in a "V"and a shorter, more rigid crankshaft.

FLAT FOUR
In cars such as the VW Beetle, the cylinders are in two flat banks. The engine is wide, but cool air can reach the cylinders so easily that water cooling is not always needed.

ROTARY ENGINE
Instead of pistons and cylinders, the "Wankel" rotary engine has a pair of three-cornered "rotors." These rotate inside a chamber, drawing in fuel, squeezing it until it is ignited, then expelling the burned gases, in one continuous movement. Rotary engines are smooth and compact, but expensive and often unreliable.

Rotor

Spark plugs

Inlet

Exhaust

Wankel rotor shaft

How the engine works

GASOLINE AND AIR is a dangerous mixture. Even the tiniest spark is enough to make it erupt into flame in an instant – which is why an engine works. Inside the cylinders, this deadly mixture is squeezed by the piston to make it even more ready to catch fire – and is then ignited by an electrical spark. It bursts into flame with almost explosive speed and expands so violently that it drives the piston back down the cylinder. It is this downward plunge of the piston – the "power stroke" – that spins the crankshaft and gives the engine its power. In nearly all car engines, this power stroke occurs once for every four times the piston goes up and down – which is, of course, why these engines are called "four-stroke" engines.

Exhaust "manifold," which channels waste gases and heat toward the exhaust pipe

Inlet valve

CROSS-SECTIONS
To show how the engine works, these two cross-sections (right and far right) were made by slicing across an engine as below. The engine is fairly advanced, with fuel injection (p. 49) and double overhead camshafts – that is, it has two camshafts at the top of the engine above the cylinder head, one for the inlet valves and one for the exhaust.

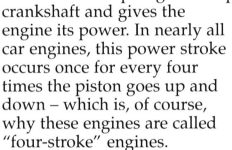

Generator

Oil filter

Section 1   Section 2

Balance weight

IN BALANCE
Notice how the crankshaft balance weights are directly below the piston when it is at the top of its stroke. This helps swing the piston down again for the next stroke.

THE CAMSHAFT
Along each camshaft are four lobes, or cams: one for each valve. As the cam rotates, each cam pushes its valve open in turn. Since the camshaft turns half as fast as the crankshaft, each valve opens once for every two revolutions of the crankshaft.

Camshaft for inlet valves

Fuel meter to insure that just the right amount of fuel is injected into the cylinders (p. 49)

Fuel injector sprays gasoline into the air streaming through the air intake

Air intake

ABOUT TO FIRE
Here the piston is at the top of the cylinder, about to start its power stroke. Both valves are closed to seal in the mixture during combustion.

Waterways through which cooling water is pumped to carry heat away from the cylinders

HOT STUFF
The burning fuel releases huge amounts of energy. Barely a third of this energy can be used to drive the car; the rest is waste heat. Much of the heat goes straight out the exhaust; the rest is carried away by the engine's cooling system.

Oil temperature sensor

LUBRICATION
Oil is pumped around the engine continuously to keep a thin film of oil between all moving parts and stop them rubbing together.

SECTION ONE

The four-stroke cycle

While the engine is running, every cylinder goes through the same sequence of events, called the four-stroke cycle, hundreds of times a minute. The power stroke occurs in each cylinder only once for every two turns of the crankshaft. But the cylinders in a 4-cylinder engine fire one after another. So there is always a power stroke in one of them.

Induction: piston descending

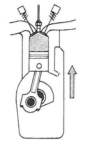

Compression: piston rising

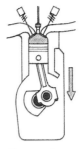

Power: piston descending

Exhaust: piston rising

THE CYCLE

The cycle begins with the "induction" stroke. The inlet valve opens and the piston slides down the cylinder, sucking in the fuel and air mixture (the "charge"). Then follows the "compression" stroke, when the valve snaps shut, trapping the charge in the cylinder, and the piston rises, squeezing it into an ever smaller space. When the piston is nearly at the top, the spark flares and the charge bursts into flame. Expanding gases drive the piston back down for the "power" stroke. Near the end of the stroke, the exhaust valve opens. Hot gases stream out, pushed by the piston as it rises again. When the piston reaches the top of its "exhaust" stroke, the cycle begins again.

VALVE TIMING

When the engine is running at 1,000 rpm – that is, just ticking over – the valves open for barely a twentieth of a second each time. In this split second, the cylinder must fill with fuel and air, so the valve must open and shut at precisely the right times – which is why the shape of each cam is crucial.

Camshaft for exhaust valves

Electrical leads to spark plugs

Exhaust

Exhaust valve

HIGH COMPRESSION

The more the charge is squeezed by the rising piston, the better it burns. Many high performance engines have a high "compression ratio" to boost power – which means that the pistons squeeze a lot of fuel into a tiny space.

Specially shaped air intake to insure that air flows into the cylinders quickly

Spark plug

Piston rings insure airtight seal around the pistons

Flywheel

Piston in lowest position, known as "bottom dead center"

SHORT STROKE

In old cars, tall and narrow cylinders meant the piston had a long way to travel up and down – so the engine could only run slowly. Modern cylinders are stubbier and the piston's "stroke" is much shorter – so the engine can run much faster.

POWER BLOCKS

Car engines vary in size and look, but nearly all depend on the four-stroke cycle. Nevertheless, in the 30 years that separate the 6-liter Ford V8 of the late 1950s (above) from the competition Renault·V10 (below), engines have improved considerably in both power and economy – through the use of new, lighter materials, improved fuel supply and ignition, and better valve gears.

Big end bearing

Oil channel through crankshaft

Crankshaft

SECTION TWO

Inside the engine

TAKE AN ENGINE APART and you will find that it is really quite simple inside. You will see the drum-shaped pistons that ride up and down, pushing and pulling on steel connecting rods to turn the crankshaft. You will see the crankshaft itself, the strong zigzag rod that drives the car's wheels as it turns. You will see the trumpetlike valves that let fuel into the cylinders and the exhaust gases out. And you will see the solid engine block and cylinder head that hold it all in place. But though the parts are simple, they must be incredibly tough to withstand the heat and stress. Temperatures reach a ferocious 3,100°F (1700°C) inside the cylinders, and the pistons have to bear pressures of up to 16 tons. All of the parts must be accurately made, too, for the engine to run smoothly and well.

Air filter

Carburetor

Spark plugs and leads

Gasoline pump

Generator

BLOCK HEAD
The cylinder head is basically a big block of metal that seals the top of the cylinders. There are slots for the valves bored through it and tunnels to carry fuel and exhaust to and from the cylinders. Little dishes, cut into the underside, form the combustion chambers (p. 42).

Oil filler

Inlet ports (2)   Rocker cover   Exhaust ports (4)

Cylinder head

OLD FAVORITE
Until front-wheel-drive cars became popular in the 1980s, most engines and their external components looked much like this.

Water pump

Inlet manifold to pipe new fuel to the cylinders

Manifolds

Exhaust manifold to carry waste gases away

PIPEWORK
The "manifolds" are the branching metal pipes that carry the fuel and air mixture into the engine and the exhaust gases away.

OM 114-1V

Engine block

BORED RIGID
The engine block is strong and heavy; it has to be, for the cylinders are bored through it, and the block has to stand up to tremendous heat and pressure. Also bored through the block are holes for cooling water and oil to circulate, and, in older engines, for the valve pushrods.

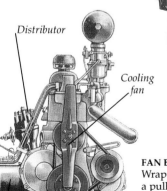

Distributor

Cooling fan

Oil filter

Timing chain cover

FAN BELT
Wrapping around a pulley on the crankshaft end, the rubber "fan belt" drives the water pump and fan, and the generator.

Oilpan

OIL BATH
After a few thousand miles of driving, the oil in the oilpan gets thin and black with dirt. It must be replaced with fresh oil in order to lubricate the engine properly.

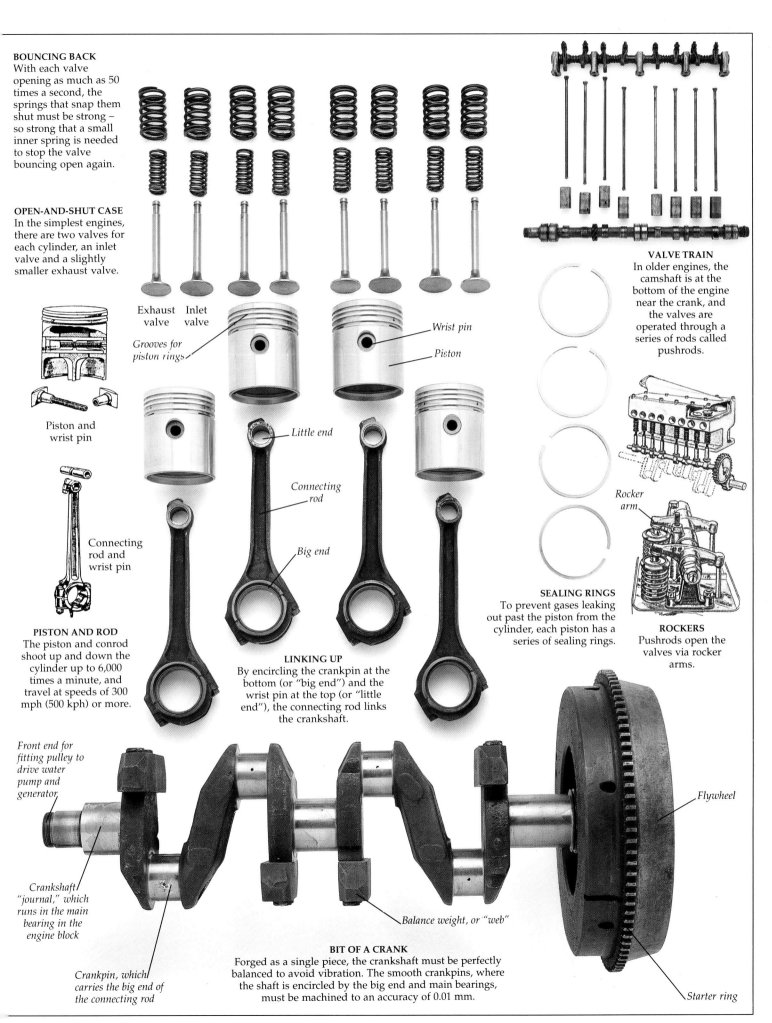

BOUNCING BACK
With each valve opening as much as 50 times a second, the springs that snap them shut must be strong – so strong that a small inner spring is needed to stop the valve bouncing open again.

OPEN-AND-SHUT CASE
In the simplest engines, there are two valves for each cylinder, an inlet valve and a slightly smaller exhaust valve.

Exhaust valve　Inlet valve

Piston and wrist pin

Grooves for piston rings

Wrist pin

Piston

VALVE TRAIN
In older engines, the camshaft is at the bottom of the engine near the crank, and the valves are operated through a series of rods called pushrods.

Little end

Connecting rod

Connecting rod and wrist pin

Big end

Rocker arm

SEALING RINGS
To prevent gases leaking out past the piston from the cylinder, each piston has a series of sealing rings.

ROCKERS
Pushrods open the valves via rocker arms.

PISTON AND ROD
The piston and conrod shoot up and down the cylinder up to 6,000 times a minute, and travel at speeds of 300 mph (500 kph) or more.

LINKING UP
By encircling the crankpin at the bottom (or "big end") and the wrist pin at the top (or "little end"), the connecting rod links the crankshaft.

Front end for fitting pulley to drive water pump and generator

Flywheel

Crankshaft "journal," which runs in the main bearing in the engine block

Balance weight, or "web"

BIT OF A CRANK
Forged as a single piece, the crankshaft must be perfectly balanced to avoid vibration. The smooth crankpins, where the shaft is encircled by the big end and main bearings, must be machined to an accuracy of 0.01 mm.

Crankpin, which carries the big end of the connecting rod

Starter ring

Fuel and air

By a happy coincidence, gasoline was discovered in 1857 – just two years before Étienne Lenoir built the first internal combustion engine (p. 6). Most car engines have run on gasoline ever since. Although other fuels will work – cars have even run on the methane gas given off by manure – gasoline has proved by far the most practical. However, no engine runs well if the gasoline is not fed in as a very fine spray, mixed with air in precisely the right proportion. A fuel mixture over-rich in gasoline burns like a wet firecracker, and gasoline is wasted. A "lean" mixture, on the other hand, contains so little gasoline that all of it is burned up far too soon to give a powerful push on the piston. So since the days of the pioneers, most cars have had some form of "carburetor" to feed the engine with the right fuel mixture. Carburetors work reasonably well and are cheap to make. But, for a more accurately metered fuel supply, many sportier cars now have "fuel injectors" instead.

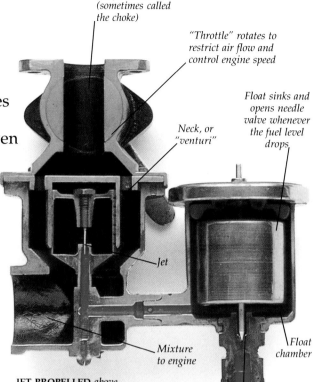

Air flows in here (sometimes called the choke)

"Throttle" rotates to restrict air flow and control engine speed

Float sinks and opens needle valve whenever the fuel level drops

Neck, or "venturi"

Jet

Mixture to engine

Float chamber

JET PROPELLED *above*
This early carburetor, cut in half to show the inside, looks very different from those of today (right). Yet it works in much the same way. Like soda through a straw, gasoline is sucked from a little reservoir called the float chamber by air streaming through the neck of the carburetor. It emerges in a fine spray through a thin tube, or "jet," and flows with the air into the engine.

Needle valve controlling fuel supply from the pump

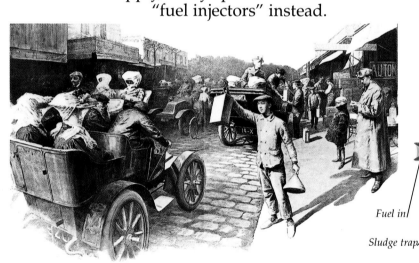

Fuel out

Pump piston

Fuel in

Sludge trap

Pump lever worked up and down as the crankshaft rotates

FUEL SHOP *above*
In the early days, gasoline had to be bought in 2-gallon (10-liter) cans and poured into the tank through a funnel.

FILL IT UP, PLEASE
Cans soon gave way to pumps that drew gasoline from an underground tank. The first were hand-operated and delivered fuel in fixed amounts from a glass dispenser. By the 1920s (below), filling stations had mechanical pumps with flow meters.

BACK TO FRONT *right*
A pump draws gasoline from the car's tank to fill the carburetor float chamber.

LEAD POWER *right*
In the 1920s, tinkering with the carb was one way of improving performance. Far better, though, was to add lead to the gasoline, first tried in 1923. The more the fuel charge is compressed, the better the engine performs (p. 45). But too much makes the charge "detonate" or explode violently rather than burn smoothly, damaging the engine. Lead in gasoline allowed high compression without detonation and so better performance. It worked so well that for 60 years, nearly all cars ran on gasoline with lead added in varying proportions or "octane ratings". Only recently did unleaded gasoline come back as people realized how bad lead is for health.

VARIABLE JET

In this carburetor, a tapered needle and a piston insure that the fuel-air mixture is right, no matter how fast the engine is running. The needle controls how much fuel sprays from the jet and the piston controls how much air flows through the neck of the carburetor. Since they both move up and down together, the mixture stays constant.

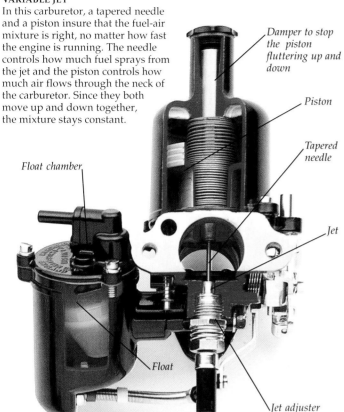

Damper to stop the piston fluttering up and down

Piston

Tapered needle

Float chamber

Jet

Float

Jet adjuster

DOUBLE BARREL

Many high performance cars have carburetors with two "chokes", like this Italian Weber. With two chokes, fuel can flow that much faster into the engine – especially if each is as broad and open as these are.

Choke

FUEL INJECTION

Carburetors rely on the engine to suck in as much fuel as it needs; fuel injectors deliver the exact amount the engine should have. The injectors are like syringes that squirt gasoline into the air intake for each cylinder. A complicated metering system insures that each dose is just right.

Turbo power

Turbochargers first showed their real potential on racing cars in 1978; now they are used on many high-performance road cars to boost power. Like superchargers, they work by squeezing extra charge into cylinders.

SELF-PROPELLED

Unlike superchargers, which are belt-driven, the rotor vanes of a turbo are spun by the exhaust as it rushes from the cylinders. As the vanes spin they turn another rotor in the inlet which forces in the extra charge.

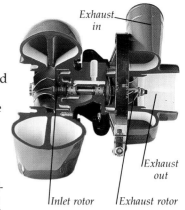

Exhaust in

Exhaust out

Inlet rotor   *Exhaust rotor*

SPECIAL VANES

Because the turbo's vanes spin around extremely fast and get very hot, they have to be carefully engineered.

HORN BLOWER

The turbo's inlet duct broadens out like a horn to build up the air pressure.

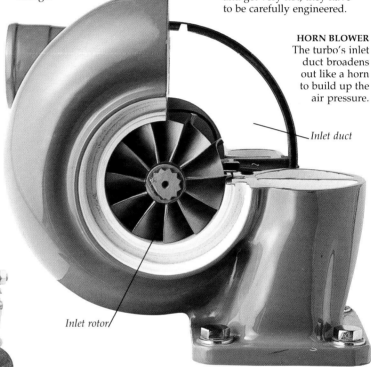

Inlet duct

Inlet rotor

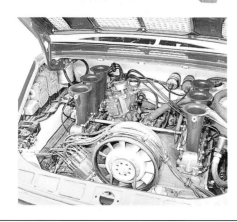

Cable from accelerator pedal pulls here to open throttle flaps

Jet

Throttle flap

Choke

THE THROTTLE

Feed a lot of fuel into the engine and it runs fast; feed in a little and it runs slow. So the accelerator pedal controls the car's speed by varying how much fuel is fed to the engine. With carburetors, the pedal turns a flap called the throttle, which opens and shuts to vary the flow of air (and fuel) through the carburetor.

The vital spark

THE SPARK PLUG MAY BE SMALL, but it is vital. It is the spark plug that ignites the fuel charge to send the piston shooting down the cylinder. It is actually just part of a powerful electrical circuit, and the twin points of the plug – the electrodes – are simply a gap in the circuit. Ten, 25, even 50 times a second, the circuit is switched on, and the current sizzles across the gap like a flash of blue lightning to ignite the charge. A huge current is needed – at least 14,000 volts – for the spark to leap the gap. Yet the car's battery only gives 12 volts. So the current is run through a coil, with thousands of windings of copper wire, to boost it dramatically for an instant. The massive current is then sent off to the correct cylinder by the "distributor". For the engine to run well, it must spark in the cylinder at exactly the right time. A spark that comes too early catches the fuel charge before it is completely compressed by the rising piston – so it burns unevenly. A spark that comes too late wastes some of the power of the charge. Some cars still have the traditional "points" to time the spark; most now have electronic "pointless" systems.

HEAVING IT INTO LIFE
Before the days of electric starters, motorists had to start their cars by hand. Ideally, a mighty swing or two on the crank was enough to send the engine spluttering into life. But strained muscles were all too common.

Plugs may have changed . . .

BUTTON START *left*
The electric starter motor – first seen on a Cadillac in 1911 – was considered a real boon for women drivers.

KEY START *right*
Carmakers soon added a key switch to the electric starter button – when drivers realized that anyone could jump into the car and drive off!

OLD SPARK *above*
Up until the 1930s, most cars used a "magneto" rather than a coil to provide the ignition voltage. The magneto was a magnet that spun between wire coils to generate a huge current. This is the control box.

CAR ELECTRICS *right*
A car will not run without a good electrical system. Electricity is needed to start the engine, to fire the ignition, and to power the lights, windshield wipers, and other accessories. Electrical systems have become much more complicated over the years but still retain the same basic elements as in this 1930s diagram.

Side light   Spark plugs   Fuses   Light switches

Dipping head light

Interior light

Starter motor   Battery

Generator   Distributor   Coil   Rear lights

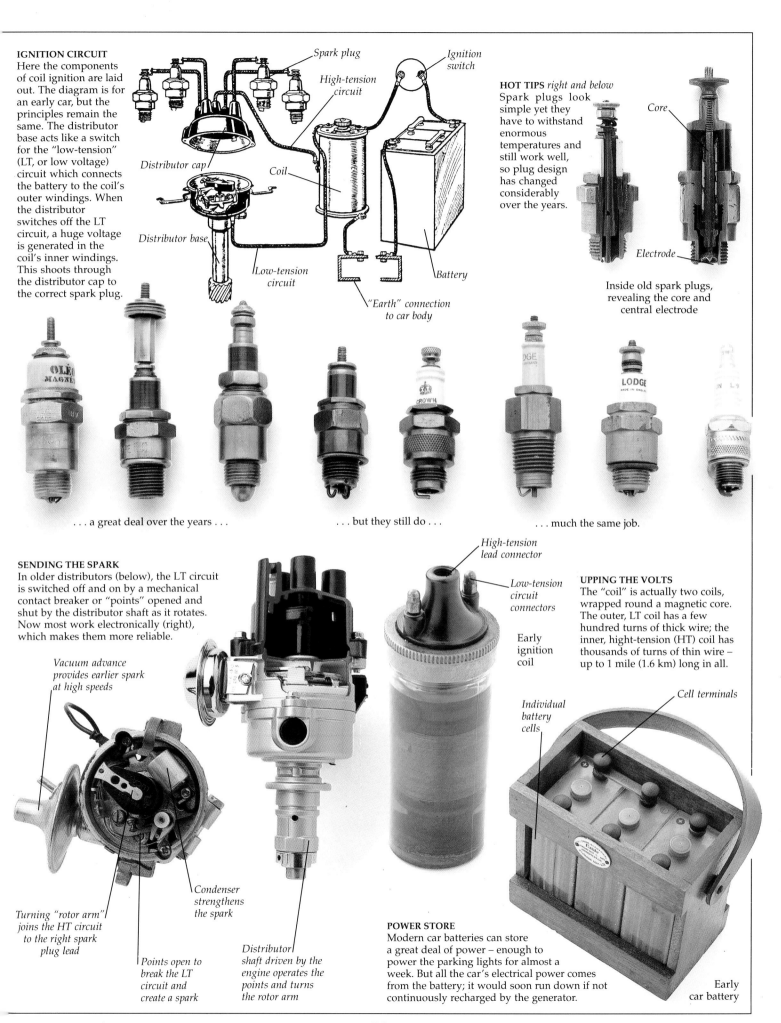

IGNITION CIRCUIT

Here the components of coil ignition are laid out. The diagram is for an early car, but the principles remain the same. The distributor base acts like a switch for the "low-tension" (LT, or low voltage) circuit which connects the battery to the coil's outer windings. When the distributor switches off the LT circuit, a huge voltage is generated in the coil's inner windings. This shoots through the distributor cap to the correct spark plug.

Spark plug

High-tension circuit

Ignition switch

Distributor cap

Coil

Distributor base

Low-tension circuit

Battery

"Earth" connection to car body

HOT TIPS *right and below*
Spark plugs look simple yet they have to withstand enormous temperatures and still work well, so plug design has changed considerably over the years.

Core

Electrode

Inside old spark plugs, revealing the core and central electrode

. . . a great deal over the years . . .   . . . but they still do . . .   . . . much the same job.

SENDING THE SPARK

In older distributors (below), the LT circuit is switched off and on by a mechanical contact breaker or "points" opened and shut by the distributor shaft as it rotates. Now most work electronically (right), which makes them more reliable.

Vacuum advance provides earlier spark at high speeds

Turning "rotor arm" joins the HT circuit to the right spark plug lead

Condenser strengthens the spark

Points open to break the LT circuit and create a spark

Distributor shaft driven by the engine operates the points and turns the rotor arm

High-tension lead connector

Low-tension circuit connectors

Early ignition coil

UPPING THE VOLTS

The "coil" is actually two coils, wrapped round a magnetic core. The outer, LT coil has a few hundred turns of thick wire; the inner, hight-tension (HT) coil has thousands of turns of thin wire – up to 1 mile (1.6 km) long in all.

Cell terminals

Individual battery cells

POWER STORE

Modern car batteries can store a great deal of power – enough to power the parking lights for almost a week. But all the car's electrical power comes from the battery; it would soon run down if not continuously recharged by the generator.

Early car battery

The drive train

I<small>N THE VERY FIRST CARS</small>, the engine was linked more or less directly to the driving wheels. Nowadays, the engine turns the wheels through a series of shafts and gears called the transmission, or drive, and every car has a gearbox. Cars need gearboxes because engines work well only when running at certain speeds. With no gearbox, the car too could only go at certain speeds. It could start off briskly, perhaps, or cruise swiftly along the highway – but not both. What the gearbox does is change how fast the wheels turn relative to the engine. To drive the wheels faster or slower, the driver selects a different gear – while the engine stays running in the same speed range. But it is not just a question of speed. Extra effort is needed to get the car moving, to accelerate, and to drive uphill. The slower ("high ratio") gears provide this extra effort by concentrating more of the engine's power into each turn of the wheel. The faster gears are for economical high-speed cruising.

THE CLUTCH
The engine's flywheel drives the gearbox via the disc-shaped "clutch plate." The clutch plate and flywheel are usually pressed firmly together and rotate as one.

ENGINE AND GEARBOX
The gearbox is bolted to the end of the engine, with the clutch in between. During gear changes, the driver presses the clutch pedal to pull the clutch plate back from the flywheel and temporarily disconnect the engine.

Clutch

"Universal" joints allow the shaft to hinge up and down

Transmission tunnel

CHAINED UP
Many early cars had a chain drive, just like a bicycle chain. It was simple but effective, and flexed easily up and down as the carriage bounced along.

REAR-WHEEL DRIVE
Until recently, nearly all cars were driven by the rear wheels, and the transmission ran back from the engine right under the length of the car.

Gearbox

Propeller shaft

Final drive

REAR ENGINE
With the engine at the back, the famous Volkswagen Beetle's gearbox was at the back, too, between the rear wheels. The car had no rear axle. Instead the wheels were driven by short drive shafts which emerged at right angles from the gearbox.

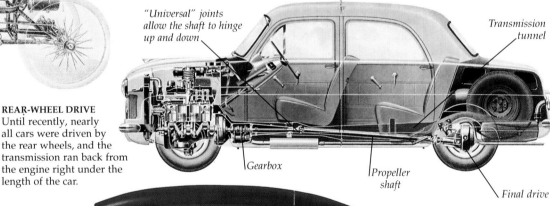

Gearbox

Gear change lever

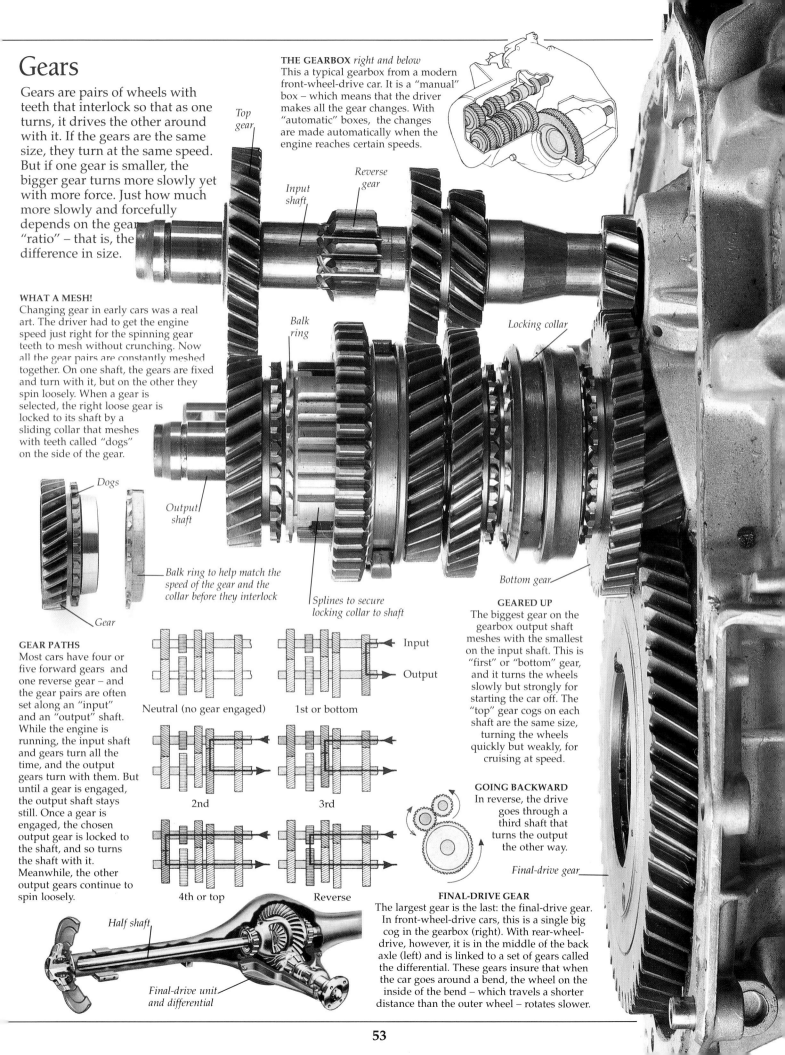

Gears

Gears are pairs of wheels with teeth that interlock so that as one turns, it drives the other around with it. If the gears are the same size, they turn at the same speed. But if one gear is smaller, the bigger gear turns more slowly yet with more force. Just how much more slowly and forcefully depends on the gear "ratio" – that is, the difference in size.

THE GEARBOX *right and below*
This a typical gearbox from a modern front-wheel-drive car. It is a "manual" box – which means that the driver makes all the gear changes. With "automatic" boxes, the changes are made automatically when the engine reaches certain speeds.

Top gear

Input shaft

Reverse gear

Balk ring

Locking collar

Dogs

Output shaft

Gear

Balk ring to help match the speed of the gear and the collar before they interlock

Splines to secure locking collar to shaft

Bottom gear

WHAT A MESH!
Changing gear in early cars was a real art. The driver had to get the engine speed just right for the spinning gear teeth to mesh without crunching. Now all the gear pairs are constantly meshed together. On one shaft, the gears are fixed and turn with it, but on the other they spin loosely. When a gear is selected, the right loose gear is locked to its shaft by a sliding collar that meshes with teeth called "dogs" on the side of the gear.

GEAR PATHS
Most cars have four or five forward gears and one reverse gear – and the gear pairs are often set along an "input" and an "output" shaft. While the engine is running, the input shaft and gears turn all the time, and the output gears turn with them. But until a gear is engaged, the output shaft stays still. Once a gear is engaged, the chosen output gear is locked to the shaft, and so turns the shaft with it. Meanwhile, the other output gears continue to spin loosely.

Neutral (no gear engaged)

1st or bottom

Input

Output

2nd

3rd

4th or top

Reverse

GEARED UP
The biggest gear on the gearbox output shaft meshes with the smallest on the input shaft. This is "first" or "bottom" gear, and it turns the wheels slowly but strongly for starting the car off. The "top" gear cogs on each shaft are the same size, turning the wheels quickly but weakly, for cruising at speed.

GOING BACKWARD
In reverse, the drive goes through a third shaft that turns the output the other way.

Final-drive gear

FINAL-DRIVE GEAR
The largest gear is the last: the final-drive gear. In front-wheel-drive cars, this is a single big cog in the gearbox (right). With rear-wheel-drive, however, it is in the middle of the back axle (left) and is linked to a set of gears called the differential. These gears insure that when the car goes around a bend, the wheel on the inside of the bend – which travels a shorter distance than the outer wheel – rotates slower.

Half shaft

Final-drive unit and differential

Smoothing the ride

CARS WERE FIRST GIVEN SPRINGS to cushion passengers from bumps and jolts; with the solid tires and rutted roads of the early days, springs were really needed. Pneumatic tyres and tarred roads have since made life much more comfortable. Even so, traveling by car would still be painful without springs to soften the ride. Yet springs are far more than just cushions. A car's suspension – its springs and dampers (shocks)– is fundamental to the way it stops, starts, and goes around corners. Without it, the car would leap dangerously all over the road – which is why modern suspension is so carefully designed.

Leaf springs

Fitted to horse carts long before cars were invented, leaf springs are the oldest form of car suspension. They are made from curved strips or "leaves" of steel, bound together by metal bands. They bend whenever the car hits a bump, but soon spring back to their original shape.

BW-37

Leaf spring for each wheel

CART TO CAR
On horse carts, only the body was carried on the springs; on cars, the chassis and engine was too – otherwise it would all have quickly shaken to pieces.

Eye for affixing spring to the main structure of the car

Rear axle usually clamped here with U-shaped bolts

Metal band to hold leaves together

More leaves for extra strength in center

Semi-elliptic (front)

Semi-elliptic (rear)

Three-quarter elliptic

LEAF FORMS
Most leaf springs were bow-shaped or "semi-elliptical" but there were many other types in the early days. Cantilevers, with the axle attached to the end of the spring rather than the middle, were popular for luxury cars.

Cantilever

CROSS-SPRING
The 1908 Ford Model T's suspension was quite unusual at the time. Most cars then had four springs running lengthwise, one for each wheel. The cost-conscious Model T (pp. 16–17) had just two, running across the car at front and back. It tended to roll and sway, but worked – even in the 1960s, some sports cars had very similar systems.

Front suspension consisting of single leaf spring which bends upward whenever the car rides over a bump

Single central mounting point for spring makes the car prone to roll and sway

SPRINGS AND SHOCKS
Shock absorbers should really be called "dampers", for it is the springs that "absorb the shock" as the car hits a bump; the shocks damp down the springing and stop the springs from bouncing the wheels long afterwards. Ideally, the wheels would follow the bumps exactly while the car stayed perfectly level.

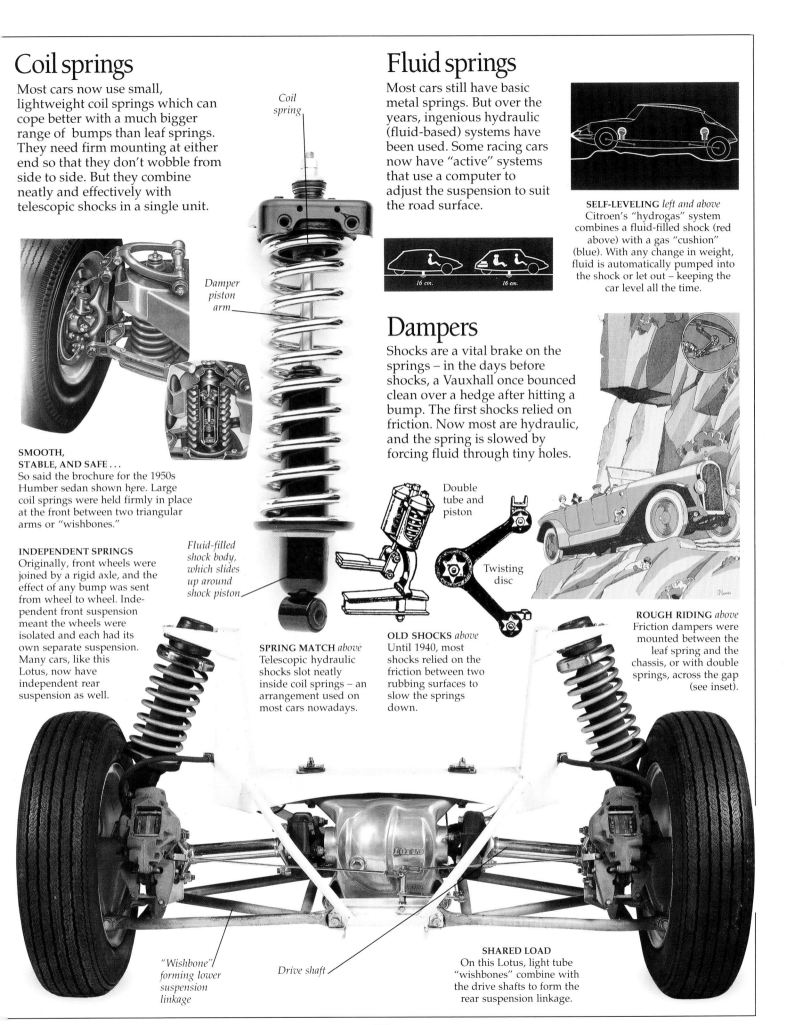

Coil springs

Most cars now use small, lightweight coil springs which can cope better with a much bigger range of bumps than leaf springs. They need firm mounting at either end so that they don't wobble from side to side. But they combine neatly and effectively with telescopic shocks in a single unit.

Coil spring

Damper piston arm

SMOOTH, STABLE, AND SAFE . . .
So said the brochure for the 1950s Humber sedan shown here. Large coil springs were held firmly in place at the front between two triangular arms or "wishbones."

INDEPENDENT SPRINGS
Originally, front wheels were joined by a rigid axle, and the effect of any bump was sent from wheel to wheel. Independent front suspension meant the wheels were isolated and each had its own separate suspension. Many cars, like this Lotus, now have independent rear suspension as well.

Fluid-filled shock body, which slides up around shock piston

SPRING MATCH *above*
Telescopic hydraulic shocks slot neatly inside coil springs – an arrangement used on most cars nowadays.

Fluid springs

Most cars still have basic metal springs. But over the years, ingenious hydraulic (fluid-based) systems have been used. Some racing cars now have "active" systems that use a computer to adjust the suspension to suit the road surface.

16 cm.   16 cm.

SELF-LEVELING *left and above*
Citroen's "hydrogas" system combines a fluid-filled shock (red above) with a gas "cushion" (blue). With any change in weight, fluid is automatically pumped into the shock or let out – keeping the car level all the time.

Dampers

Shocks are a vital brake on the springs – in the days before shocks, a Vauxhall once bounced clean over a hedge after hitting a bump. The first shocks relied on friction. Now most are hydraulic, and the spring is slowed by forcing fluid through tiny holes.

Double tube and piston

Twisting disc

OLD SHOCKS *above*
Until 1940, most shocks relied on the friction between two rubbing surfaces to slow the springs down.

ROUGH RIDING *above*
Friction dampers were mounted between the leaf spring and the chassis, or with double springs, across the gap (see inset).

"Wishbone" forming lower suspension linkage

Drive shaft

SHARED LOAD
On this Lotus, light tube "wishbones" combine with the drive shafts to form the rear suspension linkage.

Stopping and steering

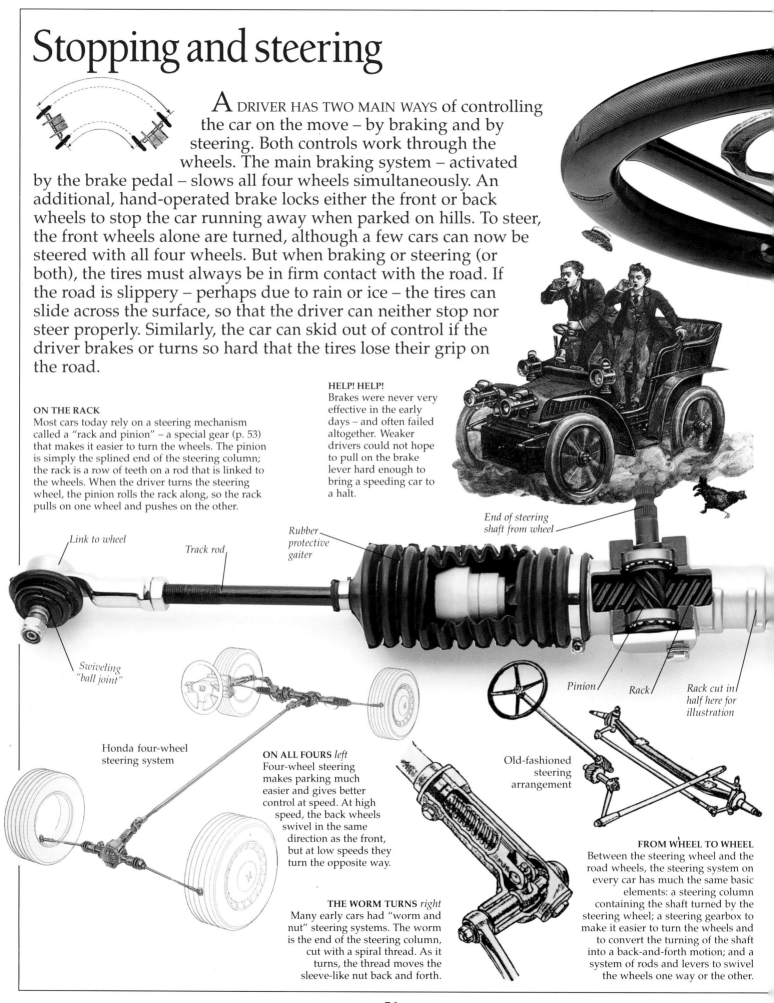

A DRIVER HAS TWO MAIN WAYS of controlling the car on the move – by braking and by steering. Both controls work through the wheels. The main braking system – activated by the brake pedal – slows all four wheels simultaneously. An additional, hand-operated brake locks either the front or back wheels to stop the car running away when parked on hills. To steer, the front wheels alone are turned, although a few cars can now be steered with all four wheels. But when braking or steering (or both), the tires must always be in firm contact with the road. If the road is slippery – perhaps due to rain or ice – the tires can slide across the surface, so that the driver can neither stop nor steer properly. Similarly, the car can skid out of control if the driver brakes or turns so hard that the tires lose their grip on the road.

ON THE RACK
Most cars today rely on a steering mechanism called a "rack and pinion" – a special gear (p. 53) that makes it easier to turn the wheels. The pinion is simply the splined end of the steering column; the rack is a row of teeth on a rod that is linked to the wheels. When the driver turns the steering wheel, the pinion rolls the rack along, so the rack pulls on one wheel and pushes on the other.

HELP! HELP!
Brakes were never very effective in the early days – and often failed altogether. Weaker drivers could not hope to pull on the brake lever hard enough to bring a speeding car to a halt.

End of steering shaft from wheel

Link to wheel

Track rod

Rubber protective gaiter

Swiveling "ball joint"

Pinion

Rack

Rack cut in half here for illustration

Honda four-wheel steering system

ON ALL FOURS *left*
Four-wheel steering makes parking much easier and gives better control at speed. At high speed, the back wheels swivel in the same direction as the front, but at low speeds they turn the opposite way.

Old-fashioned steering arrangement

THE WORM TURNS *right*
Many early cars had "worm and nut" steering systems. The worm is the end of the steering column, cut with a spiral thread. As it turns, the thread moves the sleeve-like nut back and forth.

FROM WHEEL TO WHEEL
Between the steering wheel and the road wheels, the steering system on every car has much the same basic elements: a steering column containing the shaft turned by the steering wheel; a steering gearbox to make it easier to turn the wheels and to convert the turning of the shaft into a back-and-forth motion; and a system of rods and levers to swivel the wheels one way or the other.

56

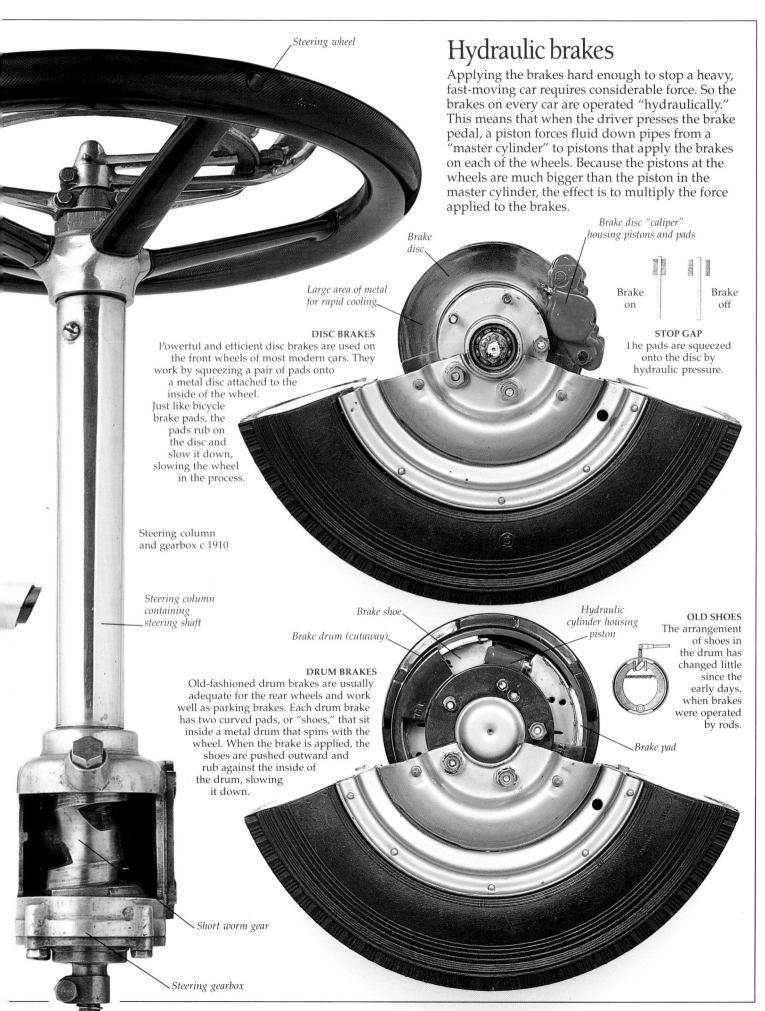

Hydraulic brakes

Applying the brakes hard enough to stop a heavy, fast-moving car requires considerable force. So the brakes on every car are operated "hydraulically." This means that when the driver presses the brake pedal, a piston forces fluid down pipes from a "master cylinder" to pistons that apply the brakes on each of the wheels. Because the pistons at the wheels are much bigger than the piston in the master cylinder, the effect is to multiply the force applied to the brakes.

Steering wheel

Brake disc

Large area of metal for rapid cooling

Brake disc "caliper" housing pistons and pads

Brake on

Brake off

STOP GAP
The pads are squeezed onto the disc by hydraulic pressure.

DISC BRAKES
Powerful and efficient disc brakes are used on the front wheels of most modern cars. They work by squeezing a pair of pads onto a metal disc attached to the inside of the wheel. Just like bicycle brake pads, the pads rub on the disc and slow it down, slowing the wheel in the process.

Steering column and gearbox c 1910

Steering column containing steering shaft

Brake shoe

Brake drum (cutaway)

Hydraulic cylinder housing piston

OLD SHOES
The arrangement of shoes in the drum has changed little since the early days, when brakes were operated by rods.

DRUM BRAKES
Old-fashioned drum brakes are usually adequate for the rear wheels and work well as parking brakes. Each drum brake has two curved pads, or "shoes," that sit inside a metal drum that spins with the wheel. When the brake is applied, the shoes are pushed outward and rub against the inside of the drum, slowing it down.

Brake pad

Short worm gear

Steering gearbox

Changing wheels

A CAR WHEEL has a demanding role to play. It needs a good airtight rim to hold the tire in place. It must be strong, too, to bear the car's weight. And it has to be tough to stand up to the forces of braking, acceleration, and road bumps. Above all, though, a car wheel has to be as light as possible, for easy starting and stopping, and to keep the car's "unsprung weight" (p. 55) to a minimum. To meet these demands, wheels have evolved steadily since the pioneering days, when wheels were big simply to give the car sufficient clearance over rutted roads. The first car wheels were adapted either from horse carts and were very heavy, or they came from bicycles and were weak. The car wheels of today are made from pressed steel or light alloys and are small, light, and strong.

HURRY, THERE, JAMES!
Carrying a spare wheel in case of a flat was still such a new idea in 1912 that it was a major selling point for wheel and tire manufacturers like Dunlop.

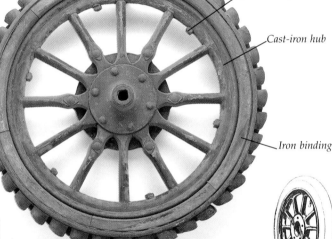

Detachable wooden rim pieces, or "felloes"

Cast-iron hub

Iron binding

Hollow steel pressing

Splined hub for quick wheel change

RIGHT WHEEL
Horse-cart origins are unmistakable in this World War I truck wheel. The spokes are cast-iron, but the rim is wooden. The wheel is immensely heavy, but strong enough to carry heavy guns. Wheels like this, and the bolt-on wheel to the right, were called "artillery" wheels.

Bolt-on hub for quick wheel change

Five-bolt hub mounting

BOLT-ON, BOLT-OFF
Flat tires were common in the early days, so the launch of the Sankey wheel in 1910 was a godsend for drivers. It could be unbolted and replaced with a spare in minutes. Made of pressed steel, it was strong and light compared with wooden wheels.

WIRED UP
For many years, cars used either Sankey-type steel wheels or wire wheels descended from the bicycle. Early wire wheels were very light and the spokes absorbed some road shocks. But the simple radial pattern of spokes meant they were not very strong. On larger wheels the spokes would bend and "whip" at speed.

Simple radial spokes prone to "whip"

Treadless tire for minimum resistance

BIG WHEEL *above and right*
This tire fitted one of the giant wheels of Malcolm Campbell's land-speed record-breaking "Bluebird" of 1935 (see inset right). Such big wheels gave the car tremendous speed over the ground before the engine reached its rev limit.

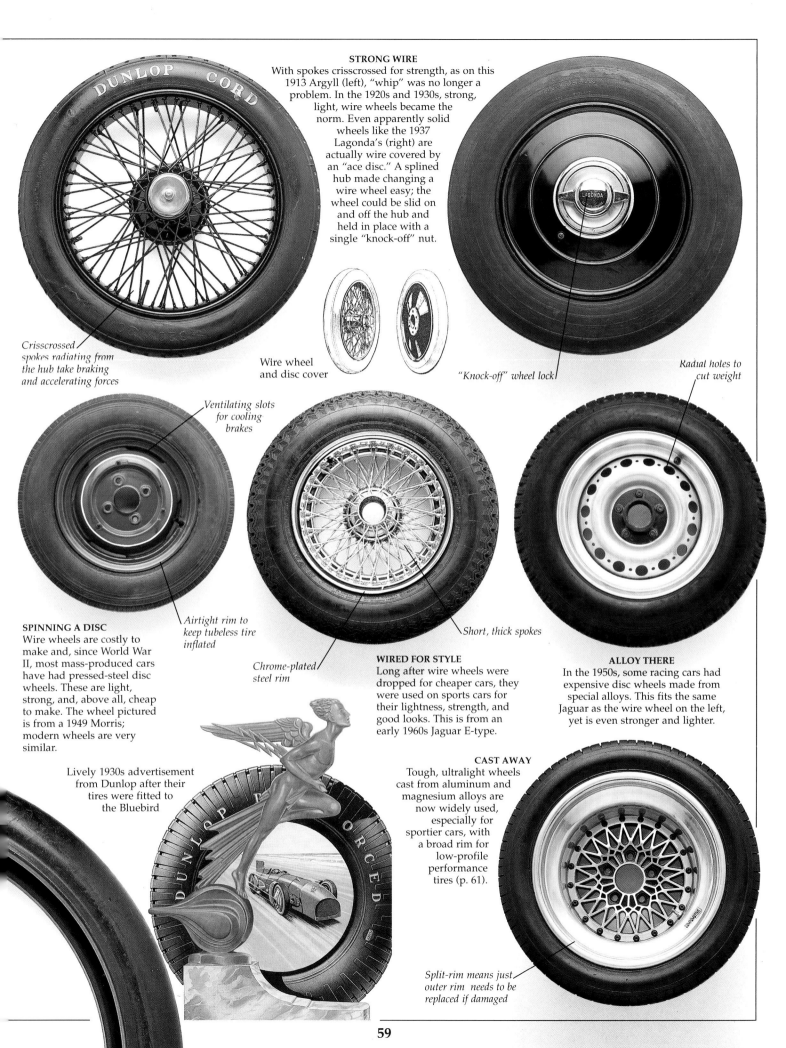

STRONG WIRE
With spokes crisscrossed for strength, as on this 1913 Argyll (left), "whip" was no longer a problem. In the 1920s and 1930s, strong, light, wire wheels became the norm. Even apparently solid wheels like the 1937 Lagonda's (right) are actually wire covered by an "ace disc." A splined hub made changing a wire wheel easy; the wheel could be slid on and off the hub and held in place with a single "knock-off" nut.

Crisscrossed spokes radiating from the hub take braking and accelerating forces

Wire wheel and disc cover

"Knock-off" wheel lock

Radial holes to cut weight

Ventilating slots for cooling brakes

SPINNING A DISC
Wire wheels are costly to make and, since World War II, most mass-produced cars have had pressed-steel disc wheels. These are light, strong, and, above all, cheap to make. The wheel pictured is from a 1949 Morris; modern wheels are very similar.

Airtight rim to keep tubeless tire inflated

Chrome-plated steel rim

Short, thick spokes

WIRED FOR STYLE
Long after wire wheels were dropped for cheaper cars, they were used on sports cars for their lightness, strength, and good looks. This is from an early 1960s Jaguar E-type.

ALLOY THERE
In the 1950s, some racing cars had expensive disc wheels made from special alloys. This fits the same Jaguar as the wire wheel on the left, yet is even stronger and lighter.

Lively 1930s advertisement from Dunlop after their tires were fitted to the Bluebird

CAST AWAY
Tough, ultralight wheels cast from aluminum and magnesium alloys are now widely used, especially for sportier cars, with a broad rim for low-profile performance tires (p. 61).

Split-rim means just outer rim needs to be replaced if damaged

Riding on air

GOOD TIRES ARE VITAL for safety and performance. Unless the tires "grip" securely on every road surface – when it is wet, when it is dry, on rough roads and on smooth – the car cannot stop, corner, or even accelerate effectively. Tires must also give a comfortable ride, run easily, and wear well. They have improved dramatically over the years, and modern "pneumatic" (air-filled) tires usually do this well, as long as they are in good condition. Careful design of the strengthening cords and webbing keeps the tire the right shape, no matter how it is squashed or pulled. The tread (the pattern of grooves) pushes water out of the way and keeps the tire in contact with the road.

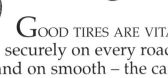

MICHELIN MAN
One of the oldest tire manufacturers of all is Michelin, a French company. "Bibendum," the Michelin Man made out of Michelin tires, is their famous trademark.

ANOTHER FLAT!
A flat tire once meant a roadside repair.

BRUTE FORCE
There was no spare wheel, so the tire had to be levered forcefully off the wheel rim, and the inner tube repaired.

TIRE AID
Once cars carried a spare wheel, the wheel could be swapped and the flat repaired later by a professional.

Rubber knobs to stop the wheel sliding and spinning on mud roads

Bumps to improve traction a little

Grooves angled in direction of rotation to aid traction on hills

Primitive tread pattern

Long channels let water flow quickly out from under the middle of the tire

SOLID RUBBER c 1915
The first tires were solid rubber. They gave a hard ride, but never punctured and were used on trucks long after cars went pneumatic.

CUSHION TIRE c 1903
Long used on bicycles, pneumatic tires were first fitted to a car in 1895. They gave a much softer ride and soon replaced solid tires.

EARLY TREAD c 1906
Smooth early tires skidded wildly on damp roads. So drivers tried leather wheel covers and different tread patterns.

DUNLOP c 1909
Early pneumatic tires had an inner tube and were narrow. They were also pumped up to high pressure to help keep them on the rim.

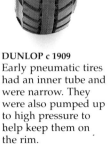

BALLOON TIRE c 1930
By 1930, cars were using wider "balloon" tires that ran at much lower pressure than earlier tires and gave a softer, smoother ride.

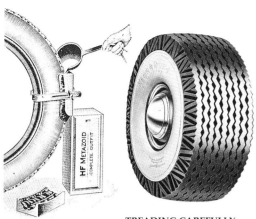

LITTLE FOOTPRINT
Only a tiny area of the tire touches the road so tread design is crucial.

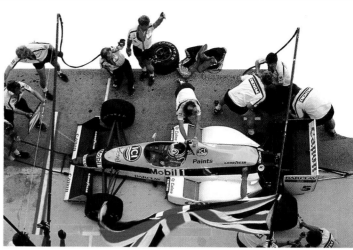

RE-TIRING
When early tires went flat, motorists often repaired them by "vulcanizing" with a sulfur mixture.

TREADING CAREFULLY
A tire's tread provides channels for water to flow out quickly and safely from under the tire, where it might otherwise reduce grip. It also gives plenty of edges for extra "bite" on the road.

WEBS AND CORDS
Rubber tires are reinforced by a network of nylon, rayon, or steel cords and webbing.

THE TIRE FOR THE JOB
Racing cars use the tire appropriate to the conditions – treadless "slicks" for dry tracks, tires with different treads for wet. Tires for road cars are a compromise to suit all kinds of conditions.

Side channels allow water near the edges to flow quickly out the side

Little incisions in the tire mop up water like a sponge

Water can accumulate in small ponds before it drains away

Tires have become wider and more squat ("low profile") to increase the area of tire in contact with the road for good grip

Slicks get extra grip as the rubber compound gets hot and sticky during the race

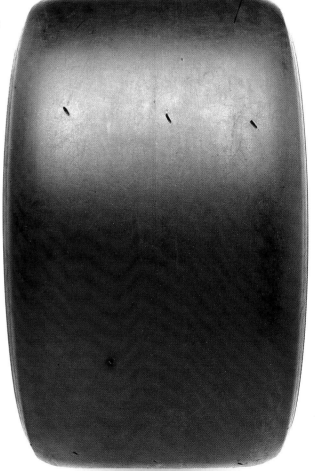

TUBELESS TIRE c 1947
In the postwar years, strong, broad, airtight wheel rims made an inner tube unnecessary. Now low-pressure, "tubeless" tires are almost universal.

RADIAL-PLY c 1972
In earlier tires, strengthening cords ran diagonally across the tire ("cross-ply"). Now most cars use "radial-ply" tires with cords running radially out from the wheel's center.

RACING SLICK
In dry weather, modern racing cars use huge, smooth tires called "slicks" to put as much rubber as possible in touch with the track for good grip.

Marques and makes

IN THE EARLY DAYS, HUNDREDS OF COMPANIES, large and small, made cars. In 1913, there were 200-odd different car "marques" (makers' names) in the U.S. alone. Each marque had its own ornament, emblem, or label to distinguish its cars from the rest. These emblems were status symbols, and were often beautifully made from hand-painted enamel or even precious metals. But as mass-production made cars cheaper, more and more of the smaller companies were swallowed up by the giants or driven out of business altogether. Many of the emblems shown here are a poignant reminder of marques long since vanished – forgotten names such as Chalmers, Bean, Swift, and Stutz. Cars still have emblems today, but they are generally much plainer.

DRAGONFLY
Ornaments became so popular in the 1920s that many owners had them specially made. The exquisite glass hood ornaments of the French jeweler René Lalique were famous. This dragonfly, like many "Laliques," is hollow. It glows magically when lit from underneath as intended.

Austin (Great Britain)

Swift (Great Britain)

Peugeot (France)

Dragonfly "Lalique"

Paige (U.S.)

ABC (Great Britain)

Chalmers (U.S.)

Sunbeam (Great Britain)

Buick (U.S.)

Oldsmobile (U.S.)

Rover (Great Britain)

Bean (Great Britain)

Fiat (Italy)

Wolseley Siddeley
(Great Britain)

Ferrari (Italy)

Morris (Great Britain)

Hupmobile (U.S.)

MG (Great Britain)

Crossley (Great Britain)

Haynes (U.S.)

Rolls-Royce (Great
Britain)

"Spirit of Ecstasy"
ornament

TOP MARQUE
Perhaps the most famous of all
the vanished marques, Bugatti, of
France, made superb, stylish cars
in the 1920s and 1930s. The
company's emblem, bearing
designer Ettore Bugatti's
distinctive "EB" logo, and
the classic horseshoe
radiator are among
the best known of all
motoring hallmarks.

Bugatti cars
and radiator

Case (U.S.)

BADGE OF DISTINCTION
Of all hood ornaments, few are
more famous than Rolls-Royce's
"Spirit of Ecstasy," which has
adorned the hoods of their cars
since 1911. This statuette, along
with the distinctive, temple-
shaped radiator grille and the RR
emblem, make Rolls-Royces
instantly recognizable.

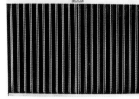
Rolls-
Royce
grille

Unic (France)

Stutz (U.S.)

Constantinesco
(France)

Did you know?

AMAZING FACTS

Could a traffic jam be music to your ears? Most American car horns honk in the musical key of F. American legend George Gershwin was among the first composers to incorporate the sound of actual car horns in his 1928 symphony, *An American in Paris*. The four horns that sound at the beginning of the work evoke a busy city street.

Hong Kong traffic jam

The world's first speeding ticket was issued in Great Britain in 1896, to Walter Arnold. Mr. Arnold was fined a shilling for doing 8 mph in a 2-mph (3 km/h in a 13-km/h) zone. The first documented American speeding ticket was issued to New York taxicab driver Jacob German in 1899.

In 1903, on a $50 bet, Dr. Horatio Nelson Jackson (with his partner Sewall Crocker and his goggles-wearing dog, Bud) became the first person to make a transcontinental car journey. At the time, there were only 150 miles (241 km) of paved roads in the US. During the 65 days it took him to travel from San Francisco to New York in his 20-horsepower Winton touring car, nearly everything that could go wrong, did. Cowboys pulled him out of sand with their lariats, people sent him miles out of the way just so their relatives could see a "newfangled" automobile, and his car broke down constantly.

Horatio Jackson, Sewall Crocker, and Bud

The very first traffic light (a revolving, gas-powered lantern that flashed red and green lights) was installed in London in 1868, before the advent of automobiles. In 1920, a version of the traffic light that copied railroad signals appeared in Detroit, Michigan. But after witnessing a number of accidents on the chaotic streets of Cleveland, Ohio, African-American inventor Garrett Augustus Morgan set out to bring some order to the roads. In 1923 he patented a T-shaped pole unit with three positions: Stop, Go, and All Stop. The third signal halted all bicycle, animal-drawn wagon, and car traffic so pedestrians could cross.

The first automobile insurance policy in the United States was issued by Travelers Insurance in Buffalo, New York, in 1898. The policy cost $11.25 and covered the liability costs involved in colliding with a horse or horse-drawn vehicle, up to $10,000.

In 1935, the world's first parking meters appeared in Oklahoma City, Oklahoma. The meters were created by Carl Magee to help solve the city's congestion problem, as city workers vied with shoppers and day trippers for the best downtown parking spots. Today, there are an estimated 5 million parking meters in use in the United States alone.

Buckle up for safety! In 1963, front seat safety belts become standard in cars, and shoulder belts became standard in the 1968 model year. But it was not until 1984 that New York became the first state to pass a law requiring the use of safety belts for all passengers.

Early meter

Modern New York State license plate

In 1901, New York became the first state to require license plates for automobiles. The first plates were not issued by the state; instead, the driver had to make his own (usually out of cardboard) and display it in the vehicle. The plates featured a number assigned by the state, and the car owner's initials. Two years later, the first state-manufactured plates (similar to what we use today) were issued in Massachusetts.

In 1995, federal speed-limit controls were lifted in the United States, leaving states in charge of setting limits. Montana does not have a numerical speed limit on non-Interstate roads; drivers must operate their cars at a "reasonable" speed.

Dude, where's my car? In 2004 the insurance industry reported that the most stolen car models are the Cadillac Escalade (a luxury SUV) and the Nissan Maxima (often stolen for its prized high-intensity headlights). What car should you buy if you don't want it stolen? The least-stolen models are the full-size Buick LeSabre and Park Avenue and the Ford Taurus station wagon.

The first car wash opened in Detroit in 1914. The car was pushed by hand through a merry-go-round-like circle, as people stood with buckets and sponges at the ready to wash the car. The first fully automated car wash was established in 1946, also in Detroit.

A recent survey by a major automobile insurance company found that 26 percent of Americans who responded "love" their car; 9 percent claim their car is the "center of my life." The same survey found that 67 percent of Americans have nicknames for their cars. Girl's names are more popular than boy's names, with Betsy topping the list.

QUESTIONS AND ANSWERS

Interstate sign

Q How many automobiles are there in the world?

A In the 1970s, there were an estimated 200 million cars on the road worldwide. In 2000, that figure jumped to close to 450 million cars, and the numbers are on the rise. China is the world's fastest-growing auto market. Over the last two years, auto production and sales increased at a rate of more than 50 percent, and that trend is expected to continue. For example, Beijing was the first city in China to top the 2-million vehicle mark. By 2008 (in time for the Summer Olympics) there will be 3.8 billion cars there.

Q How many cars are manufactured each year?

A Global auto manufacturers build approximately 60 million new cars and trucks every year. Each vehicle needs a unique VIN (vehicle identification number), in the same way that newborns in many countries are given social security numbers. But so many cars are being built that manufacturers worry they will run out of these 17-digit numbers by the year 2010.

Q How many cars are there in the United States today?

A The number of vehicles registered in the United States recently surpassed 200 million for the first time. Of these, approximately 125 million are passenger cars and 75 million are trucks. In 2003, the number of cars in the U.S. per household (1.9) exceeded the number of drivers (1.7) for the first time.

Q What are the world's largest automotive groups today?

A The five major manufacturing groups are: General Motors, Ford, DaimlerChrysler, Toyota, and Volkswagen. GM is the largest. This Detroit-based company produces more than 8 million vehicles a year. GM car brands sold in the United States include Cadillac, Chevrolet, Buick, Oldsmobile, Pontiac, and Saturn.

Q How many miles do cars travel each year?

A On average, each car in America is driven 12,000 miles a year, but it is taking people much longer to get from A to B. Traffic congestion is increasing in the United States, in both urban and suburban areas. Since 1982, the U.S. population has grown nearly 20 percent, but the time an average rush-hour commuter spends in traffic has grown by 236 percent. That means a commuter in a typical American city spends an extra 62 hours a year (the equivalent of about one and a half working weeks) stuck in traffic.

Q How many roads are there in the United States?

A From quiet country lanes to traffic-clogged city streets, there are more than 4 million miles (6.4 million km) of public roads in the United States. Laid end to end, they would circle the globe more than 157 times, or go to the moon and back more than eight times. The Department of Transportation classifies roads by function. More than half the total road miles in the U.S. are local roads, providing access to homes, farms, and businesses.

Toll plaza at the Golden Gate Bridge, San Francisco

Q What is the longest highway in the Interstate System? What is the shortest?

A The longest highway in the Interstate System is I-90; its 3,085 miles (4,900 km) stretch from Seattle to Boston. The shortest is I-97, an 18-mile (30-km) highway running between Baltimore and Annapolis, Maryland.

Q How many miles of toll roads are there in the United States?

A There are more than 4,788 miles (7,700 km) of toll roads, bridges, and tunnels in the United States.

Q What are the latest car accident statistics?

A Despite air bags and other safety features, some 42,000 people are killed in automobile crashes each year in the United States, and another 3 million are injured.

Record Breakers

BEST-SELLING CAR
The Toyota Corolla—more than 25 million have rolled off assembly lines worldwide.

MOST EXPENSIVE CAR
A 1954 Mercedes Benz W 196 sold in 1990 for $24 million dollars. Its current owner is believed to have bought the car for half that amount in the late 1990s.

LARGEST PRODUCTION CAR
The Bugatti Royale Type 41 (Golden Bugatti), built in 1927, was 22 ft (6.7 m) long.

LARGEST PRODUCTION PICKUP TRUCK
International Truck and Engine Corp's CXT is 9 ft (2.7 m) high, 8 ft (2.4 m) wide, and 21 ft (6.4 m) long.

SMALLEST PRODUCTION CAR
The Mercedes Benz Smart car, arriving in the U.S. in 2006, is 8 ft (2.4 m) long.

FASTEST PRODUCTION CAR
The Bugatti Veyron speeds from 0 to 60 mph in 3 seconds and can reach 279 mph (449 km/h). The price? $1.4 million dollars.

Bugatti Royale

Cars and culture

THE INVENTION OF THE AUTOMOBILE routinely makes the lists of top-ten inventions that have changed our lives. But the culture of cars has its own history, just as interesting as the history of the automobile itself. Cars have become symbols of freedom and independence, statements of identity, and objects of desire. They also embody the promises of technology and the dream of a better future. As the number of cars increased on the road, so did the roadside attractions. Here is a guide to some of the cultural markers that have emerged in the Automobile Age.

Cars at the first filling station, c. 1907

FILL 'ER UP (1907)
In the early 1900s, there were no gas stations. Motorists had to hunt down fuel at a hardware or general store. But as more people bought cars, there was a greater demand for places to buy fuel. In 1907, John McLean, a manager at a Standard Oil of California (now Chevron) factory in Seattle, Washington, got an idea: he put a water heater on a platform, attached a garden hose to dispense gasoline, and added a gauge that measured the fuel flowing into a customer's tank. With a canopy to shelter the station attendant and shelves for oils and greases, the first filling station was open for business.

HOP TO IT (1921)
By 1920 there were 8 million automobiles on American roads; chances are, some of those people were hungry. Texas businessman J.G. Kirby figured out a way to get food to people in their cars by inventing the first drive-in restaurant, the Pig Stand, in 1921. Customers would pull up to the lot and an agile "car hop" would leap onto the running board of their automobile to take their food order. Need more ketchup? A flick of the headlights would summon the car hop again. The drive-in restaurant craze lasted long into the 1960s.

A car hop serves food to a customer

HIT THE HIGHWAY (1925)
In the early days of motoring, road markings were chaotic. Motorists had to look for colored bands on telephone poles or randomly placed signs to ensure they hadn't driven astray. Crafty businesses could "relocate" highways to ensure traffic passed through their towns. The U.S. Federal Aid Highway Act in 1925 did away with named roads, replacing them with uniform numbers and the shield sign still in use today. Although road signs are not international, their reliance on images rather than text makes them easier to understand. In general, the use of red indicates a warning or prohibition, while blue draws attention to a useful feature (such as a parking garage). A circle is usually a restriction, while a square or rectangle gives guidance. A triangle usually shows priority (as in the Australian sign above, telling drivers to give way to kangaroos).

Australian highway sign

STOP AND SHOP (1927)
The first convenience store opened in Dallas, Texas, in 1927. Local ice supplier "Uncle Johnny" Jefferson Green realized that people needed to buy staples like bread, milk, and eggs after regular grocery stores closed. Convenience stores kept long hours (typically 7 AM until 11 PM) and were typically open seven days a week. Within a few years, "drive in" markets dotted the country; people could shop for essentials without leaving their cars. In the 1950s, as Americans with bigger cars and better roads flocked to the suburbs, there was a huge boom in convenience stores, which quickly supplanted the neighborhood grocery store.

CRANKING UP THE TUNES (1929)
Without Paul Galvin of Illinois, you couldn't sing along to music in your car. Galvin invented the first car radio in 1929. The next year, running low on working capital and desperate for financial help, Galvin hoped to convince the local banker that he was on to a good thing by installing a radio in the banker's car for a demonstration. Unfortunately, the radio triggered a fire under the car's hood. Galvin overcame that hurdle and his Motorola radio soon became America's leading brand.

AT THE DRIVE-IN (1933)
New Jersey native Richard Hollingshead had two interests in life: movies and cars. He was looking for a way to combine them when he came up with the idea for the drive-in movie. Experimenting in his own driveway, Hollingshead mounted a projector on the hood of his car, and projected movies onto a screen nailed to trees in his backyard. A radio behind the screen provided sound. In 1933, he opened his first theater in Camden, NJ.

Texas drive-in, c.1949

LITTLE TREES (1952)

That new car smell wears off quickly; since 1952 many motorists have relied on the Car-Freshner's Little Trees (in the United Kingdom and Australia, they are called Magic Trees). These cardboard pine trees, manufactured in Watertown, New York, are the most popular car air fresheners in the world today, sold in more than 26 different countries across the globe.

Little Trees

U.S. Interstate sign (left); Thai highway sign (center); German autobahn sign (top right)

A NIGHT AT THE INN (1952)

A road-weary motorist in the 1920s had few choices about where to stop for the night. Camping was the only option for the budget-minded. But in the 1920s, a new "motor hotel" emerged: the motel. These were often mom-and-pop operations on the outskirts of a town, consisting of a single building with interconnecting rooms facing a parking lot and a motel office. Their anonymity made them ideal places for shady activities; Bonnie and Clyde frequently used motels as hideouts. In 1952, Kemmons Wilson, upset by the wildly different standards he found in motels on a family vacation, founded the first Holiday Inn in Memphis, Tennesee. His goal was to offer standardized motel rooms, at a reasonable, family-friendly price. The chain's success all but ended the mom-and-pop era and led to the creation of several other motel chains.

Neon Holiday Inn sign

INTERSTATE HIGHWAY (1954)

As a young man, future American president Dwight D. Eishenhower traveled from Washington, D.C., to San Francisco. Like many people making the same trip, he encountered dirt roads and crumbling bridges. Congress worked to establish an east-west, north-south system of interstate highways; shortly after Eisenhower became president in 1953, he authorized funding for the system. The Federal Highway Acts of 1954 and 1956 set a budget for a network of 41,012 miles (66,000 km) of minimum two-lane highways. The interstate system now stretches over 46,380 miles (74,600 km). Interstates carry one- or two-digit numbers. North-south routes have odd numbers; east-west routes have even numbers. For north-south routes, numbering begins in the west. So, I-5 runs along the Californian Central Valley, while I-95 runs along the East Coast. Interstates that travel around a city center such as I-495, circling our nation's capital, carry three-digit numbers.

RO-RO CAR FERRIES (1960S)

Car ownership soared in the 1950s, and more and more people were packing up the family car to hit the open road. But crossing bodies of water in a car was troublesome. Cars had to be hoisted onto cargo ships. In the early 1960s, roll-on, roll-off car ferries were in service in Europe and other parts of the world. A driver could simply drive right inside the ferry, and drive off at the other end, with a very quick turnaround. The ferries revolutionized European transport.

DRIVE-THRU DINING (1975)

The first McDonald's drive-thru (short for "drive-through") opened in Sierra Vista, Arizona, in 1975. In the three-day grand opening ceremony, every tenth car got a free order, and one lucky person won a year's supply of Big Macs. The original drive-thru was demolished in the late 1990s to make way for a new restaurant in the chain.

A customer picks up a food order at a drive-thru

Find out more

IT MAY BE A FEW YEARS YET before you are ready to get behind the wheel, but there are plenty of other ways to find out more about cars. Visit your local science center to learn about how cars work, or visit an automotive factory to see how a car is built. Many excellent museums across the country are devoted to automobiles and automotive history. If motor sports are more your speed, go see a race.

FORD'S LIFETIME AND LEGACY
Visit a replica of Henry Ford's workshop, where he tinkered on his first car, as well as the first Model T factory, and Ford's childhood home—all at Greenfield Village, an incredible living history museum in Dearborn, Michigan. You can even take a spin in a restored Model T car or a Model A truck. Ford's grandson enjoys a vintage ride in this picture.

LOOK INSIDE AN ENGINE
Don't know your axle from your elbow? Your local science and technology center may have exhibits dedicated to the inner workings of a car. Exhibits might include a cutaway of an internal combustion engine like this one, helping to explain the "nuts and bolts" of how cars work.

USEFUL WEB SITES

www.ford.com
The home of the Ford Motor Company and its related brands.

www.daimlerchrysler.com
An on-line "museum" helps you explore the heritage of this company.

www.gm.com
The history and the latest news on the General Motors family of brands.

www.toyota.com
The official web site of the Toyota Motor Corporation.

www.vw.com
The Internet home of Volkswagen of America, and a link to Volkswagen sites worldwide.

TAKE A FACTORY TOUR
Some automobile manufacturing companies offer factory tours, so visitors can see the manufacturing process up-close. The Ford Motor Company, for example, conducts tours of its historic Rouge Factory in Dearborn, Michigan. The Rouge is the largest single industrial complex in the world. When the plant is in full production, visitors cross a catwalk suspended above the factory floor, experiencing all the heat and noise of the assembly line. Check the Internet for a tour near you.

VISIT AN AUTO SHOW

Before auto manufacturers roll out their new models, you can get a sneak preview at an auto show. These vast events held in many major cities bring all of the latest developments in the automotive world under one roof. You could also visit a classic car show or rally. Check the Internet or your local newspaper for details.

Places to Visit

PETERSEN AUTOMOTIVE MUSEUM, LOS ANGELES, CA
This museum dedicated to the interpretive study of the automobile and its influence on our culture and lives features more than 150 rare and classic cars, trucks, and motorcycles.

SMITHSONIAN INSTITUTION, WASHINGTON, DC
The National Museum of History and Technology contains extensive transportation exhibits. About 20 cars are on permanent display, including the 1903 Winton that was the first car driven across America.

INTERNATIONAL MOTORSPORTS HALL OF FAME AND MUSEUM, TALLADEGA, AL
This complex adjacent to the world-famous Talladega Superspeedway is a racing enthusiast's dream, with more than 100 vehicles.

SAN DIEGO AUTOMOTIVE MUSEUM, SAN DIEGO, CA
This world-class collection of cars and motorcycles is housed in a historic building in San Diego's Balboa Park.

NATIONAL CORVETTE MUSEUM, BOWLING GREEN, KY
This museum, celebrating its ten-year anniversary, is dedicated to America's sports car: the Chevrolet Corvette. You can also visit the nearby GM Corvette assembly plant.

NATIONAL AUTOMOBILE MUSEUM, RENO, NV
This unique museum features more than 200 cars from 1892 to the present day. The cars are arranged in chronological order, so you can discover more than a century of automobile history in a few hours.

NORTHEAST CLASSIC CAR MUSEUM, NORWICH, NY
More than 125 rare and fabulous classic cars are on display, including the world's largest collection of Franklin luxury cars.

ROUTE 66 MUSEUM, CLINTON, OK
Get your kicks on Route 66 at this museum dedicated to America's most famous highway.

HENRY FORD MUSEUM AND GREENFIELD VILLAGE, DEARBORN, MI
An amazing living history museum dedicated to Ford, and American invention and innovation.

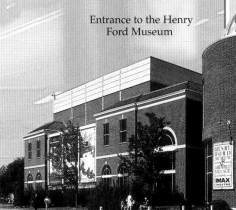

JOIN THE FAST TRACK
When you go to a car race, you can almost taste the excitement in the air. Or is that the lingering trace of all that supercharged fuel? You probably live within a short drive of some kind of auto racing, from a demolition derby to a professional NASCAR race (above). Going to a race is something you will remember long past the last victory lap.

Entrance to the Henry Ford Museum

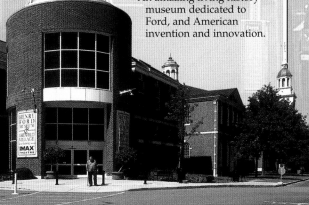

VISIT AN AUTOMOBILE MUSEUM
From the "horseless carriage" to the mega-horsepower race car, you can explore the evolution of the automobile and its impact on our culture by visiting one of the automotive museums in the box. These museums typically feature permanent collections of cars, motorcycles, trucks, and motoring ephemera. The above display of old-time cars and gas-station memorabilia is from the Simpler Times Museum, located in Tidioute, Pennsylvania.

Glossary

ACCELERATOR A mechanical device (in a motor vehicle, the gas pedal) linked to the throttle valve of the carburetor, and used to control the flow of fuel into the engine for increasing speed

AERODYNAMICS The study of airflow over and around an object and an important part of automobile design. The positive and negative lift of the airflow is studied in wind tunnels as part of the car design process. Negative lift, which presses the vehicle closer to the ground, is preferred.

ALTERNATOR A device that turns mechanical energy into electricity, providing energy for a car's electrical system

ARMATURE A wooden or wire support around which a model or sculpture is constructed. In car design, an armature is made of wood and foam, then covered in clay to make a full-size model.

AXLE The rod in the hub of a wheel on which the wheel turns

BATTERY A series of two or more electric cells arranged to produce, or store, energy. A modern car battery can store a great deal of power, but it must be constantly recharged by the generator.

BRAKE A device for applying resistance to a moving part to slow it down (for example, a car brake)

BRAKE PADS The name for the rubbing part of a brake that slows the wheel down

BRAKE SHOES In drum brakes, the curved pads that sit inside a metal drum that spins with the wheel

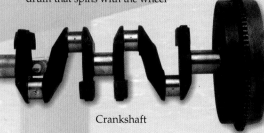

Crankshaft

CAMSHAFT A rotating shaft with a number of irregularly shaped "cams," used to open and close the engine cylinder valves, usually via push rods and rocker arms. The crankshaft drives the camshaft.

CHASSIS The structural framework of a car to which the working parts and the car body are attached

CHROME A hard, silvery metal polished to a high shine, used to make car bumpers

CLUTCH A mechanism that uses plates coated with a high-friction material to transfer power from the engine to the drive train. Manual transmission vehicles use a clutch to transfer power from the gearbox to the wheels. This word also describes the pedal used to engage the device.

COG One in a series of projections on a toothed wheel. Cogs are used in gearboxes.

COIL SPRING A bar of resilient metal wound into a spiral that may be extended or compressed without losing its shape permanently. Coil springs are particularly important in car suspension.

COMBUST To burn up. The combustion chamber is the space where the fuel-air mixture begins to burn.

COMPRESSION RATIO A high compression ratio describes a high-performance engine that boosts its power by compressing fuel into a small space.

CONVERTIBLE The name for any car with a folding roof

CRANKCASE A boxlike casing for the crankshaft and connecting rods

CRANKSHAFT The main shaft of a car engine that carries a crank or cranks, which attach to connecting rods that transmit power from the pistons

CRUMPLE ZONE The front and rear portions of a car, designed to crumple and absorb the impact in a collision while the passenger seating area remains intact

CYLINDER The name for the tubular chamber in which a car piston works

DASHBOARD The instrument panel of a car, originally named for the board that protected the driver of a horse-drawn vehicle from splashes of mud

DISC BRAKE A type of brake in which the friction is obtained by pads forced against a disc on the wheel

DISTRIBUTOR A device in a car's engine than transmits high-voltage current in the correct sequence to the spark plugs

DRIVE Another word for the all the parts of the transmission

DRIVE TRAIN The combination of a car's components—engine, transmission, differential, hubs, shafts, gears, and clutches—that transmits the engine power to the wheels

DRUM BRAKE A type of brake in which two shoes grip the inside of the brake drum

ELECTROMAGNET A piece of soft iron or other metal, made magnetic by a current of electricity passing through a coil of wire wound around it

ENGINE A highly complex mechanical device in which power is applied to do work. Nearly all car engines get their power from the up-and-down movement of the pistons.

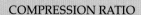

Cogs

EXHAUST The exit of gases or fluids as waste products from the cylinder of an automobile's engine. Also, the name for the system that expels these gases.

FAN A rotating device providing ventilation to the engine

FAN BELT In a car, a continuous belt that drives the alternator and the cooling fan for the radiator

FIBERGLASS A synthetic fiber made of extremely fine filaments of molten glass, used to make reinforced plastics

FLYWHEEL A rotating element attached to the rear of an engine crankshaft, to maintain uniform revolutions per minute

Grille used for cooling and decoration

FUEL INJECTOR An electronically controlled valve that introduces, under pressure, a precise amount of vaporized fuel directly into the combustion chamber

GASOLINE A light fuel used to spark ignition engines in cars. Modern gasolines are blends of petroleum liquids that are refined in several different ways and usually contain chemical additives to enhance performance.

GEARBOX A set of rotating cogged wheels called gears, connected to a shaft, which enable a car's driver to change speeds

GEARS Cogged wheels. Meshing the teeth of two gears together enables one set to rotate the other.

GRILLE An often decorative component in an air system, placed at the inlet or outlet of the airflow

HYDRAULIC Moved or operated by liquid (water or oil); for example, the hydraulic brakes in a car

IGNITION An electrical system in an engine that provides the spark that fires the air-fuel mixture in the cylinder

INTERNAL COMBUSTION ENGINE An engine that produces power from the combustion and expansion of a fuel-and-air mixture within a closed cylinder

LEVER A simple machine consisting of a rigid bar that is free to pivot on a fulcrum

MANIFOLD A fitting that connects a number of branches to a main system (as in the exhaust system of the internal combustion engine)

Gasoline pump

MANUAL TRANSMISSION A gearbox in which the driver must manually match the engine's speed to the correct gear, using a clutch and stick shift

MASS PRODUCTION The manufacture of goods (such as automobiles) in large quantities by means of machines, standardized design, and sometimes assembly lines

MUFFLER A device attached to the exhaust stack of the engine to reduce the noise of vehicle operation

OCTANE A flammable liquid hydrocarbon found in petroleum. The octane number describes the grade of gasoline and its resistance to engine knocking.

PISTON A partly hollow cylindrical part, closed at one end, fitted to each of an engine's cylinders and attached to the cranks. Each piston moves up and down in its cylinder, transmitting power created by the exploding fuel to the crankshaft via a connecting rod.

PNEUMATIC Relating to something that is moved or worked by air pressure

PULLEY A wheel over which a belt or chain passes. Pulleys can be used to change the speed of a mechanism. If a large pulley is connected by a belt to a small pulley, the small pulley pulls faster, causing an increase in speed. If a small pulley is used to drive a large one, there is a decline in speed but an increase in power.

PUSH RODS A series of rods that open valves in a camshaft through rocker arms

RACK AND PINION A type of steering system in which the wheel gear (the pinion) meshes with a toothed rack. When the steering wheel is turned, the pinion gear turns, moving the rack to the left or right, thus steering the wheels.

RADIATOR A metal device that cools the engine by dispersing heat that has been absorbed by the coolant circulating around the hot engine

RENDERING A perspective drawing of a car designer's plan for an automobile

SHOCK ABSORBER The name for any device that uses air or hydraulic pressure to dampen the up-and-down movement of a moving car

SPARK PLUG A small device that produces an electrical spark to ignite the fuel-air mixture in the cylinder

SPRING An elastic metal device that returns to its shape or position when pushed, pulled, or pressed

STARTER RING A ring with teeth that meshes with teeth on the starter motor, to spin the engine and cause it to start up

SUPERCHARGER A crank-driven air-fuel mixture compressor. It increases air pressure in the engine to produce more horsepower.

SUSPENSION A mechanical system of springs or shock absorbers connecting the wheels and axles to a car's chassis

THERMOSTAT An automatic control device used to maintain temperature at a fixed or adjustable set point

THROTTLE The device that controls the power produced by the engine at any given moment. The throttle regulates the fuel-air mixture that goes into the cylinders of the engine.

TRACTION An expression that describes the amount of grip produced by a car's tires and suspension system

TRANSMISSION The gears that transmit power from an automobile engine via the driveshaft to the axle

TURBOCHARGER A compressor or pump that pressurizes engine intake air. It forces more air into the cylinder than it could normally draw, so the engine burns more fuel and in turn produces more power.

Turbocharger

VALVE A device that can be opened and closed to allow or prevent the flow of a liquid or gas from one place to another. Most internal combustion engines use intake and exhaust valves to allow fuel-air mixture into the cylinders, and for exhaust.

VANADIUM STEEL An ultra-strong steel alloy, used in automobile manufacturing

Index

Acknowledgments

The publisher would like to thank:
The National motor Museum,
Beaulieu: pp. 6-7, 8-9, 10-11, 12-13, 14-15,
18-19, 20-21, 22-23, 24-25, 26-27, 32-33, 58-
59, 60-61, 62-63; and special thanks to
Roger Bateman, Tony Cooper, and Derek
Maidment for their help.
The Science Museum, London: pp. 30-31,
48-49, 50-51, 54-55, 56-57.
Colin Tomlinson and Mr. Parsons of Essex
Autotrim pp. 16-17, 54.
American Dream, Maidstone: pp. 28-29;
and George Flight for his valuable help.
Renault, France pp. 36-45.
Tim Jackson, Bob Gibbon, and the staff of
Renault UK for their help with pp. 36-41.
Bryn Hughes and John Gillard of Classic
Restorations, London: pp. 46-47.
Italdesign, Turin, and the Design
Museum, London: pp. 34-35.
The Carburettor Centre, London for the

variable jet and Weber carburetors on p. 49.
Lucas Automotive: pp. 51; with special
thanks to Ken Rainbow.
Karl Shone for special photography: pp.
34-35.
Peter Mann of the Science Museum or his
help with the text.
Lester Cheeseman for his desktop
publishing expertise.

Picture credits

t=top b=bottom l=left r=right c=center

Allsport: 61tr
Neill Bruce: 49tr
Jean Loup Charmet: 20bl; 23tl; 50cl; 63bc
Colorsport: 33cr; 47bl
Mary Evans Picture Library: 6bl; 8bl;12tr;
13tr; 16bl; 17tc; 18tl; 19tr, br; 21tl; 22cl; 25tr;
48cl, bl, br; 55cr; 56cr; 58tl; 59bc

Ford Motor Company: 24cr
Honda UK Ltd: 56bl
Hulton Picture Library: 52cl
Jaguar Cars Ltd: 43tr
Mansell Collection 8cl; 9cr; 14cr; 16tl
National Motor Museum: 11tr; 15tr; 24tl;
26cr; 38tr; 50br; 52tr
Quadrant Picture Library 32tl
Rolls-Royce Motor Cars Ltd: 63bc
Rover Group plc: 37TC, tr; 37br

AP Wideworld: 67tl, 68bl, 69tl
Corbis: James L. Amos 68tl; Bettmann 65bl,
66-67bc; Henry Diltz 67cl; Robert Holmes
65c; Bob Krist 68-69c; David
Madison/NewSport 69c; Museum of
History and Industry 66tl; Tim Page 67tr;
Joseph Sohm; ChromoSohm Inc. 65tr;
Keren Su 64tl
Getty Images: 67br; Time Life Pictures
64br, 66bl

University of Vermont, Special
Collections: 64bl

Jacket images: *Front:* DK Images: Dave
King/National Motor Museum, Beaulieu
(cal, tl, tr); Dave King/National Motor
Museum, Beaulieu and Rolls Royce Motor
Cars Ltd (tcr); Mike Dunning/The Science
Museum, London (tcl). Getty Images: The
Image Bank (b). *Back:* DK Images: Dave
King/National Motor Museum, Beaulieu
(bl, c, car, cfl, cl); Mike Dunning/The
Science Museum, London (cl, cra).

Illustrations by: John Woodcock

Picture research: Cynthia Hole